JAMES

THE RELATIONSHIP BETWEEN

FAITH AND WORKS

DR. DAVID JEREMIAH

Prepared by Peachtree Publishing Services

HarperChristian
Resources

James
Jeremiah Bible Study Series

© 2021 by Dr. David Jeremiah

Requests for information should be addressed to:
HarperChristian Resources, 3900 Sparks Dr. SE, Grand Rapids, Michigan 49546

ISBN 978-0-310-09180-6 (softcover)
ISBN 978-0-310-09181-3 (ebook)

HarperChristian Resources titles may be purchased in bulk for church, business, fundraising, or ministry use. For information, please email ResourceSpecialist@ChurchSource.com.

Produced with the assistance of Peachtree Publishing Services (www.PeachtreePublishingServices. com). Project staff include Christopher D. Hudson and Randy Southern

First Printing September 2021 / Printed in the United States of America

CONTENTS

INTRODUCTION TO
The Letter of James

"But be doers of the word, and not hearers only, deceiving yourselves" (James 1:22). The connection between faith and works lies at the very heart of the letter of James. The author of this short epistle is concerned not only with what we as followers of Christ *believe* but also with how those beliefs shape our *behaviors* and *actions*. James understood that a confession of faith in Christ must be reflected in our daily works—influencing the choices we make, the things we say, the priorities we pursue, the people with whom we align ourselves, and the way we respond to temptation. James' words read like a collection of wisdom instructions, much like those found in the literature of the Old Testament, and includes practical advice for putting our faith into action. He writes with the heart of a pastor-leader who wants us to demonstrate actions that will prove—to ourselves and to a watching world—that our faith is genuine and sincere.

AUTHOR AND DATE

The writer of this letter identifies himself as "James, a bondservant of God" (1:1). While many men in the New Testament are identified with this name, the leading candidates for authorship are James the son of Zebedee, a disciple of Christ (see Mark 1:19), and James "the Just," a brother of Jesus and early leader in the Jerusalem church (see Mark 6:3). The early church fathers attributed the letter to James the Just for two reasons: (1) the disciple James was martyred in AD 44, before certain issues addressed in the letter became matters of concern in the Christian community, and

(2) the wording of the letter is consistent with the speech given by James at the Jerusalem Council (see Acts 15:13–21). The Jewish orientation of the epistle, the structure of the Christian churches it addresses, and the lack of references to Gentile communities, all point to an early composition date—likely sometime in the mid to late AD 40s.

BACKGROUND AND SETTING

James is a "general" letter, addressed not to a specific church but to "the twelve tribes which are scattered abroad" (James 1:1). This likely refers to Jewish Christians who were dispersed throughout the regions of Mesopotamia and the Mediterranean. The fact that James addresses both the rich and the poor provides an idea of the diverse backgrounds of those who made up the first-century church. Many of the scattered Jews fell on hard times in foreign lands. They worked as day laborers and found themselves at the bottom of the social ladder. In contrast, a minority had achieved great financial security and social acceptance. In many areas, these two groups were part of the same Christian congregation, and tensions between the groups occasionally ran high, especially during times of famine and struggle. In his letter, James applies God's wisdom to the relationship between the "haves" and "have nots" and helps his readers understand how their interaction relates to the greater theme of faith and works.

KEY THEMES

Several key themes are prominent in the letter of James. The first theme is that *believers in Christ must persevere through trials.* James is clear that we *will* experience "various trials" and must develop the skills necessary to patiently endure through them. Such perseverance will lead to spiritual growth, give us a new perspective on our lives, and help us to see the potential for God's good work in every situation (see James 1:2–4; 5:7–12).

A second theme is that *followers of Jesus must love everyone equally.* As previously noted, the early church was comprised of those who found themselves at the top of the social and economic ladder and those who were on the lower rungs. But James holds that such differences do not matter in the family of God. All followers of Jesus must love others equally and show no favoritism or partiality based on social standing. Furthermore, James counsels the wealthier believers not to place confidence in their riches or ignore the plight of the poor, whose cries ascend to the very ears of God (see 1:9–11; 2:1–13; 5:1–6).

A third theme is that *believers in Christ must be careful with their speech.* It appears that malicious gossip was doing great harm to the early church and was damaging relationships between believers. James wanted his readers to understand the incredible power the believers' words possessed and to use their speech to build up others in love instead of tearing them down. The same tongue that praises God should never be used to curse another person. So, James offers several practical tips for how believers can control their tongues . . . instead of allowing their tongues to control them (see 1:26; 3:1–12).

A fourth theme is that *believers in Christ should practice good works.* James is perhaps best known for his teachings on how believers should balance faith and works in their lives. While he, like the apostle Paul, is clear that good works do not save a person, he is equally clear that such good works must be the natural outcome of a person's salvation. James urges his readers to embrace a personal code of morality and ethics based on loving God with everything that is within them—and loving their neighbors as themselves (see 1:21–25, 27; 2:14–26).

KEY APPLICATIONS

James offers strong pastoral counsel on how our beliefs must translate into life. As Christians, we are held to a higher standard in our conduct, speech, priorities, and relationships. It is not enough for us to have a "private" faith and just blend in with everyone else. We must stand out from the world—and demonstrate the love that Jesus has shown to us by loving others and caring for those in need. The spotlight will be especially intense on us when we face adversity and setbacks. But if we are able to maintain a God-honoring perspective in the midst of those trials, then we will make an impact on others and demonstrate God's love to them.

COUNT IT ALL JOY

James 1:1–8

GETTING STARTED

What is your typical reaction when you encounter difficulties in life?

SETTING THE STAGE

The opening words of James reveal the intended audience of the letter: "to the twelve tribes which are scattered abroad" (1:1). These "twelve tribes" refer to the people of Israel, who as far back as the eighth century BC had been dispersed to various foreign lands as a result of conquest and exile. Many of these Jews had come to believe in Jesus as the promised Messiah and were now facing severe trials as a direct consequence of placing their faith in Christ.

James' opening statement to this group of persecuted believers indicates that his intent is to encourage them and give them hope to endure. But what is surprising is the mindset that he advises them to take toward these struggles. He writes, "Count it all joy when you fall into various trials, knowing that the testing of your faith produces patience . . . let patience have its perfect work, that you may be perfect and complete, lacking nothing" (James 1:2–4).

The trials these believers were facing would have likely included poverty, discrimination, oppression, imprisonment, physical abuse (through beatings), and even the threat of death. Most of us today will not suffer from these same forms of persecution. But we all will face our share of trials—the loss of a job, a divorce, trouble with our children, financial strain, illness, or a death in the family. Whatever the case, James' words in the first eight verses of his letter are just as relevant to us today as they were for the scattered Jews some 2,000 years ago.

Now, in order to approach this opening section of James' letter with the proper perspective, we must first recognize the inevitability of suffering. Notice that James writes, "Count it all joy *when* you fall into various trials." We might like that word to say *if*, but James clearly states *when*. We cannot go from the cradle to the grave without being touched by adversity. Each of us, at some time in our lives, *will* face trials.

The second word to note is *count*. The Greek word that James uses for *count* means "to think forward." In our culture, we might say, "fast-forward." When we're in the midst of trials, our best strategy is to fast-forward in our mind to what God is up to and rejoice in what He is going to do in us in the midst of our pain. To "count it all joy" in the midst of our trials is to respond to what is going on in our lives with an intelligent appraisal of our situation. It is to look at our trial from God's perspective and recognize that, while the trial itself is not a happy experience, God is using it to produce something that will be valuable within us.

EXPLORING THE TEXT

Greeting to the Twelve Tribes (James 1:1–4)

¹ James, a bondservant of God and of the Lord Jesus Christ,
  To the twelve tribes which are scattered abroad:
  Greetings.
  ² My brethren, count it all joy when you fall into various trials,
³ knowing that the testing of your faith produces patience. ⁴ But let patience have its perfect work, that you may be perfect and complete, lacking nothing.

1. James, the author of this letter, had impeccable credentials. Not only was he the respected leader of the first-century church in Jerusalem, but he was also the brother of Jesus. Yet how does he choose to identify himself to his readers? What is James communicating to his readers by identifying himself in this way (see verse 1)?

2. The Greek word translated as *perfect* in verse 4 does not refer to sinlessness but rather to a "perfect result"—which in this case is spiritual maturity. What is James saying about the purpose of trials? How can that lead to actually rejoicing in them (see verses 2–4)?

_____

_____

_____

_____

_____

_____

_____

_____

_____

_____

_____

_____

Profiting from Trials (James 1:5–8)

⁵ If any of you lacks wisdom, let him ask of God, who gives to all liberally and without reproach, and it will be given to him. ⁶ But let him ask in faith, with no doubting, for he who doubts is like a wave of the sea driven and tossed by the wind. ⁷ For let not that man suppose that he will receive anything from the Lord; ⁸ he is a double-minded man, unstable in all his ways.

3. James recognizes that none of his readers will have achieved this state of spiritual maturity in which they are "lacking nothing" (verse 4). So, he provides some guidelines on how to take the first step along the path.

What is that first step? What promise is given to those who desire to
receive this from God (see verse 5)?

_____

_____

_____

_____

_____

_____

_____

_____

_____

4. The word that James uses for *wisdom* in verse 5 refers to an
understanding of God's ways, while the word he uses for *faith* in
verse 6 refers to a commitment to act on those ways. What happens
when a person hesitates or "doubts" in making that commitment?
What is the warning for those who are not fully committed to act on
God's ways (see verses 6–8)?

_____

_____

_____

_____

_____

_____

_____

_____

_____

_____

_____

GOING DEEPER

James is not the only New Testament writer who recognized the potential for spiritual growth in times of trial and suffering. In his letter to the believers in Rome, the apostle Paul traced a similar growth arc that could only occur as result of patient endurance through tribulations. Like James, Paul recommends what we would consider a counterintuitive attitude toward trials.

Faith Triumphs in Trouble (Romans 5:1–5)

¹ Therefore, having been justified by faith, we have peace with God through our Lord Jesus Christ, ² through whom also we have access by faith into this grace in which we stand, and rejoice in hope of the glory of God. ³ And not only that, but we also glory in tribulations, knowing that tribulation produces perseverance; ⁴ and perseverance, character; and character, hope. ⁵ Now hope does not disappoint, because the love of God has been poured out in our hearts by the Holy Spirit who was given to us.

5. Paul states that believers can have peace in the midst of trials. The phrase translated as "have access" means to approach, as if by introduction, a king's throne room. What are the benefits for believers of having been "introduced" to God by Christ (see verses 1–2)?

_____

_____

_____

_____

_____

_____

6. Paul states that we can actually "glory in tribulations." What does Paul say that trials and tribulations produce in us (see verses 3–4)? How are his words similar to those of James ?

_____

_____

_____

_____

_____

_____

_____

_____

_____

_____

_____

Spiritual growth is a lifelong process—the hard-earned result of making God-honoring decisions in all circumstances. The apostle Peter, in his first letter, offers us the following big-picture perspective of what those decisions to remain faithful eventually add up to in our lives.

A Heavenly Inheritance (1 Peter 1:6–9)

[6] In this you greatly rejoice, though now for a little while, if need be, you have been grieved by various trials, [7] that the genuineness of your faith, being much more precious than gold that perishes, though it is tested by fire, may be found to praise, honor, and glory at the revelation of Jesus Christ, [8] whom having not seen you love. Though now you do not see Him, yet believing, you rejoice with joy inexpressible and full of glory, [9] receiving the end of your faith—the salvation of your souls.

7. "Trials" refers to the ordeals we encounter in life and not necessarily things that might cause us to sin. Why should we rejoice about the trials we have endured (see verses 6–7)?

_____

_____

_____

_____

_____

_____

_____

_____

_____

8. The "salvation of your souls" refers to our glorification in heaven and the rewards we will receive there. Why will God honor us in this way (see verses 8–9)?

_____

_____

_____

_____

_____

_____

_____

_____

_____

_____

Reviewing the Story

James begins his letter by challenging conventional wisdom. Contrary to popular belief, trials and suffering are not necessarily punishments from God, nor are they random incidents of bad luck that we are helpless to do anything about. Instead, James suggests that trials are *opportunities* for spiritual growth. The key to unlocking their potential is to recognize the spiritual fruit that they are producing in us. Furthermore, when finding joy in the midst of trials proves difficult, we can ask for God's wisdom and be confident that He will respond generously.

9. How can you "count it all joy" when you face trials (see James 1:2–3)?

_____

_____

_____

_____

_____

_____

_____

10. What happens when you allow patience to do its work in your life (see James 1:4)?

_____

_____

_____

_____

_____

_____

_____

11. Why can you be confident when you ask God for wisdom (see James 1:5–6)?

_____

_____

_____

_____

_____

_____

12. Why should you strive to not be a "double-minded" person (see James 1:7–8)?

_____

_____

_____

_____

_____

_____

APPLYING THE MESSAGE

13. How have some of the trials you have endured led to greater trust in God? How have those trials resulted in greater spiritual maturity?

_____

_____

_____

_____

_____

14. What is a situation in your life right now where you especially need God's wisdom?

_____

_____

_____

_____

REFLECTING ON THE MEANING

James opens his letter with a call for believers in Christ to calculate the results of their trials. In other words, as Christians, we must take an objective look at the positive impact that the trials we are enduring are having on our lives. James points out two key benefits that trials produce.

First, trials produce durability. According to an old saying, Christians should never pray for patience because when they do, God will send them trials. The challenges we face will help us to trust in God and wait patiently on Him. Now, note that *patience* is not sitting back and letting things happen without any response. The term, as it is used in James 1:4, is active. Patience means acknowledging that even when we are going through things we do not understand, God is working in the midst of those circumstances. He may not always tell us what He is doing, but He will teach you perseverance.

Second, trials produce maturity. According to James 1:4, after durability has done its work in our lives, we become perfect and complete. Again, the word *perfect*, as used in this context, does not mean sinless but rather mature. Without the durability that comes through trials, believers cannot grow up. We cannot become mature. After we make it through a trying situation, we can look back on it and see how God worked in and through it. That realization deepens our relationship with Him and prepares us for the next trial we will face.

Our afflictions make us mature, and our maturity makes us "complete." Until we have gone through some things that hurt, we are unfinished products. This is why we can "count it all joy" when we face trials, for God is doing incredible things through them in our lives. He is strengthening us, toughening us, and making us complete.

Journaling Your Response

How can you take a more positive approach in responding to the trials and difficulties you face?

VICTORIOUS IN TRIALS

James 1:9–18

GETTING STARTED

How would you describe the difference between *trials* and *temptations*?

_____

_____

_____

_____

_____

_____

_____

_____

_____

_____

_____

_____

_____

_____

_____

SETTING THE STAGE

James has just discussed how God uses trials to help believers mature in their faith. In this next section, he will turn the discussion to the topic of *temptation*. Whereas trials are to be counted as a reason for joy, temptations are to be renounced and abandoned in the believer's life. Interestingly, in the original Greek, the word translated as *trials* and *temptations* used in James 1 is the same. Only the context reveals whether the word should refer to outward troubles or inward enticements. This one word denotes two very different meanings.

Picture this in terms of our English word for *knife*. When a murderer takes a knife to slash the flesh of his victim, it is for the purpose of destroying that person. But when a skilled surgeon uses a blade to cut the flesh, it is for the purpose of healing. In each circumstance the same blade is used, but for very different purposes. In the spiritual realm, Satan is the murderous tempter, and our Lord is the skilled surgeon. Satan tempts us to bring out the bad (see verses 13–19), while God tests us to bring out the good (see verses 1–12).

While trials and temptations are different, they do have some things in common. Without proper preparation in either case, the believer can be defeated. In other words, if we go into trials with no knowledge of what is going on (based on Scripture), we can be overcome by our trials and get so discouraged that we give up on God. Likewise, if we enter into life with no preparation for the temptations that we will face, we will quickly fall prey to the snares of sin. Nothing tests the integrity of our faith like our response to temptation.

Remember that James wrote his letter to Jewish believers who had been expelled from Israel. He knew they faced not only persecution but also enticements to sin in the nations where they were living. His message is for them to endure for Christ in all circumstances.

EXPLORING THE TEXT

The Perspective of Rich and Poor (James 1:9–13)

> [9] Let the lowly brother glory in his exaltation, [10] but the rich in his humiliation, because as a flower of the field he will pass away. [11] For

no sooner has the sun risen with a burning heat than it withers the grass; its flower falls, and its beautiful appearance perishes. So the rich man also will fade away in his pursuits.

[12] Blessed is the man who endures temptation; for when he has been approved, he will receive the crown of life which the Lord has promised to those who love Him. [13] Let no one say when he is tempted, "I am tempted by God"; for God cannot be tempted by evil, nor does He Himself tempt anyone.

---

1. James begins his discussion on temptation by addressing the enticements in a believer's life for material gain and status. His use of the word *brother* in this passage indicates that the individuals he is talking about are believers. What is the caution and warning for Christians who are looking to their material wealth for security (see verses 9–11)?

_____

_____

_____

_____

_____

_____

_____

_____

_____

_____

_____

2. In the athletic events of the day, a crown was given to the one who endured the trials and won the competition. How does James say a believer wins the "crown of life"? What does he say about the source of these challenges that we must overcome (see verses 12–13)?

_____

_____

_____

_____

_____

Loving God Under Trial (James 1:14–18)

14 But each one is tempted when he is drawn away by his own desires and enticed. 15 Then, when desire has conceived, it gives birth to sin; and sin, when it is full-grown, brings forth death.

16 Do not be deceived, my beloved brethren. 17 Every good gift and every perfect gift is from above, and comes down from the Father of lights, with whom there is no variation or shadow of turning. 18 Of His own will He brought us forth by the word of truth, that we might be a kind of firstfruits of His creatures.

3. The phrase *drawn away* can refer to physically dragging someone away against his or her will. What does this say about the damage that temptation can cause (see verses 14–15)?

_____

_____

_____

_____

_____

4. James has been clear about the source of temptation and the devastating effects it brings into a believer's life. He now contrasts those gifts of destruction with God's good and perfect gifts. How does James describe these good gifts? What purpose do these gifts serve in the life of a believer in Christ (see verses 16–18)?

_____

_____

_____

_____

_____

_____

_____

GOING DEEPER

In Paul's letter to the Philippians, he also draws on imagery of an athletic event to illustrate the kind of life that Jesus calls his followers to lead. Paul, like James, encourages believers in Christ to press on through trials to reach "the goal for the prize" that awaits them.

Press on Toward the Goal (Philippians 3:12–19)

[12] Not that I have already attained, or am already perfected; but I press on, that I may lay hold of that for which Christ Jesus has also laid hold of me. [13] Brethren, I do not count myself to have apprehended; but one thing I do, forgetting those things which are behind and reaching forward to those things which are ahead, [14] I press toward the goal for the prize of the upward call of God in Christ Jesus.

[15] Therefore let us, as many as are mature, have this mind; and if in anything you think otherwise, God will reveal even this to you. [16] Nevertheless, to the degree that we have already attained, let us walk by the same rule, let us be of the same mind.

¹⁷ Brethren, join in following my example, and note those who so walk, as you have us for a pattern. ¹⁸ For many walk, of whom I have told you often, and now tell you even weeping, that they are the enemies of the cross of Christ: ¹⁹ whose end is destruction, whose god is their belly, and whose glory is in their shame—who set their mind on earthly things.

---

5. Athletes in a race understand they have to keep focused on the road ahead and not worry about the runners that might be creeping up behind them. How does this describe the focus that Christians must have when it comes to securing victory (see verses 12–14)?

_____

_____

_____

_____

_____

_____

6. Paul is intentional in saying that he is still running the race of the Christian life—that he is continuing to press on toward the goal. What does he encourage believers to do in this regard? Why is it critical for them to stay focused on the prize (see verses 17–19)?

_____

_____

_____

_____

_____

James warns of the dangers of succumbing to temptation, noting that it "gives birth to sin; and sin, when it is full-grown, brings forth death" (1:15). Paul was likewise straightforward in warning the Corinthian believers about the dangers of submitting to temptation. In the following passage, he also addresses the issue of being too overconfident in one's resolve.

Warnings from Israel's History (1 Corinthians 10:11–13)

11 Now all these things happened to [the Israelites] as examples, and they were written for our admonition, upon whom the ends of the ages have come. 12 Therefore let him who thinks he stands take heed lest he fall. 13 No temptation has overtaken you except such as is common to man; but God is faithful, who will not allow you to be tempted beyond what you are able, but with the temptation will also make the way of escape, that you may be able to bear it.

7. Paul understood the power the sinful nature has on a person. What warning does he give to those who may be resting too comfortably in their victory in Christ (see verses 11–12)?

_____

_____

_____

_____

_____

_____

_____

_____

_____

_____

8. Paul notes that temptation is never unique to an individual. The enemy has been using temptation to compel people to sin all the way back to the Garden of Eden. What are the promises given for those who are encountering temptation (see verse 13)?

_____

_____

_____

_____

_____

Reviewing the Story

James addresses the issue of temptation in this section of his letter. He begins with a discussion of the believers' temptation to secure material wealth, warning that such material possessions will fade away and that no hope or security can ever be found in them. He encourages the believers to patiently endure temptation and to continue to pursue the crown of life that God has set before them. He compels his readers to always resist the urge to sin, noting that such behaviors only lead to death, and to instead seek the good gifts that God provides.

9. What are the lowly (the poor) and the rich instructed to "glory in" (see James 1:9–10)?

_____

_____

_____

_____

_____

10. What image does James use to warn rich believers not to pursue wealth for wealth's sake (see James 1:10–11)?

_____

_____

_____

_____

_____

_____

11. How does desire—an overwhelming lust for something—lead to spiritual death (see James 1:14–15)?

_____

_____

_____

_____

_____

_____

12. Of what should we remind ourselves when we are tempted to believe that we have earned the wealth and possessions we enjoy in this life (see James 1:16–17)?

_____

_____

_____

_____

_____

_____

APPLYING THE MESSAGE

13. How do you ensure that you are placing your trust in God and not material wealth?

_____

_____

_____

_____

_____

_____

_____

_____

_____

_____

14. What are some of the good and perfect gifts that God has provided in your life?

_____

_____

_____

_____

_____

_____

_____

_____

_____

_____

REFLECTING ON THE MEANING

James offers four principles in this section of his letter for how to be victorious over temptation instead of a victim of temptation.

The first principle is to assume responsibility for temptation. James emphasizes in verse 13 that it is not God who tempts us but our own sinful desires. If we try to blame God—or anyone else—for falling prey to temptation, we create a false narrative. We must be willing to look in the mirror and say, "The responsibility is mine."

The second principle is to anticipate the routine of temptation. James outlines Satan's four-step scheme for getting us to submit to temptation in verses 14–16. Satan starts with *enticement,* encouraging us to turn routine desires into runaway desires. Next, he uses *entrapment* to exploit our weaknesses and use the right bait to catch us. He follows this with *endorsement,* urging us to act on the temptation and commit sin against God. Finally, he uses *enslavement* to encourage us to make the sin a habit and then a lifestyle. If we don't want Satan to take advantage of us, it is vital that we understand this strategic process.

The third principle is to activate the replacement for temptation. James reminds us in verse 17 that in contrast to the evil enticements that come from *within* us, all good gifts are from God, who is *over* us. So, the way to deal with temptation is to fill our minds with good things. Instead of focusing on the temptation itself, we focus on the One who has promised to give us the victory over that temptation. We meditate on His goodness, revel in His mercy and grace, and occupy every thought with His truth.

The fourth principle is to accept the reason for our temptation. James reminds us in verse 18 that we experience temptation because of who we are. We are tempted because we are followers of Christ. So, if you struggle with temptation, be encouraged! You are being tempted because the enemy is trying to keep you from being the kind of person whom God wants you to be. But remember, you don't have to be a victim. You can be a victor! Simply focus on the Father of lights, and He will provide the way through the temptation.

JOURNALING YOUR RESPONSE

How can these principles help in your battle to overcome temptation?

LESSON *three*

DOERS OF THE WORD

James 1:19–27

GETTING STARTED

How would you describe the difference between a "hearer" and a "doer" of God's Word?

_____

_____

_____

_____

_____

_____

_____

_____

_____

_____

_____

_____

_____

_____

_____

_____

_____

SETTING THE STAGE

The Bible is readily available throughout the world. In fact, the Word of God has been translated into more than 1,800 different languages. So, for most people, the question is not whether they have *access* to God's Word but whether they will take *action* on what it says. This is a question that James takes seriously, so he concludes the opening chapter of his letter with a heartfelt appeal to give God's Word the importance that it deserves.

As James notes, this begins by taking a purposeful approach to studying Scripture. After all, anything worth doing is worth doing *right*. For example, let's say we wanted to prepare a meal for a special occasion. We wouldn't just root though the cupboards and throw together the first thing we found. No, we would start with a *plan*. We would go to the store to shop for just the right ingredients, check the recipe to see how everything should be prepared, and carefully monitor the food to make sure nothing is undercooked or overcooked. In other words, we would put in the necessary work to ensure the result was something special.

James exhorts us to approach God's Word with a similar attitude. He urges us to prepare ourselves in such a way that the Bible might have the maximum impact on us. As is the case with cooking ribs—or anything else—what we get out of studying God's Word depends on what we put into it. And what we get out of approaching Scripture with the right attitude is life-changing. We find that the truth and wisdom of God's Word naturally flows into our actions and attitudes. We become doers of the Word and not merely hearers of the Word.

EXPLORING THE TEXT

Preparing Your Heart for God's Word (James 1:19–22)

> [19] So then, my beloved brethren, let every man be swift to hear, slow to speak, slow to wrath; [20] for the wrath of man does not produce the righteousness of God.

²¹ Therefore lay aside all filthiness and overflow of wickedness, and receive with meekness the implanted word, which is able to save your souls.

²² But be doers of the word, and not hearers only, deceiving yourselves.

---

1. The triple exhortation that James employs in verse 19 reveals his deep concern about how divisiveness affects not only our relationships but also our spirits. What three attitudes must believers embrace as they prepare their hearts for God's Word (see verses 19–20)?

_____

_____

_____

_____

_____

_____

_____

2. The word translated *meekness* in verse 21 refers to humility, as opposed to an aggressive haughtiness that forces its opinions and desires on others. What happens when we approach God's Word with a sense of meekness (see verses 21–22)?

_____

_____

_____

_____

_____

_____

Be Doers of the Word (James 1:23–27)

23 For if anyone is a hearer of the word and not a doer, he is like a man observing his natural face in a mirror; 24 for he observes himself, goes away, and immediately forgets what kind of man he was. 25 But he who looks into the perfect law of liberty and continues in it, and is not a forgetful hearer but a doer of the work, this one will be blessed in what he does.

26 If anyone among you thinks he is religious, and does not bridle his tongue but deceives his own heart, this one's religion is useless. 27 Pure and undefiled religion before God and the Father is this: to visit orphans and widows in their trouble, and to keep oneself unspotted from the world.

3. James uses the analogy of a man looking into a mirror to explain the difference between a hearer and a doer of the Word. The man looks into the mirror, sees his face, and then forgets what he looks like! What point is James making here (see verses 23–24)?

4. In contrast, those who are doers of God's Word will investigate what the Bible says and then allow its teachings to influence their actions. What are some of the outward signs that such a transformation is taking place in a person's life (see verses 25–27)?

_____

_____

_____

_____

_____

_____

_____

_____

GOING DEEPER

The apostle Paul, just like James, placed a high value on not only reading the Word of God but also applying its truths to our lives. In his second letter to Timothy, he explains how the Bible can help us discern between true and false teachings. He also notes some of the benefits that we will receive when we choose to become doers rather than just hearers of the Word.

The Man of God and the Word of God (2 Timothy 3:10–17)

[10] But you have carefully followed my doctrine, manner of life, purpose, faith, longsuffering, love, perseverance, [11] persecutions, afflictions, which happened to me at Antioch, at Iconium, at Lystra—what persecutions I endured. And out of them all the Lord delivered me. [12] Yes, and all who desire to live godly in Christ Jesus will suffer persecution. [13] But evil men and impostors will grow worse and worse, deceiving and being deceived. [14] But you must continue in the things which you have learned and been assured of, knowing from whom you have learned them, [15] and that from childhood you have known

29

the Holy Scriptures, which are able to make you wise for salvation through faith which is in Christ Jesus.

[16] All Scripture is given by inspiration of God, and is profitable for doctrine, for reproof, for correction, for instruction in righteousness, [17] that the man of God may be complete, thoroughly equipped for every good work.

---

5. Paul draws a sharp contrast between the empty words of false teachers and the active faith he exhibited. What did that active faith look like in Paul's life (see verses 10–15)?

_____

_____

_____

_____

_____

_____

6. Paul lists four things in verse 16 for which Scripture is profitable. Only one of these, *doctrine*, involves knowledge. The other three involve a change of life: (1) *reproof* refers to demonstrating a truth beyond dispute, (2) *correction* refers to setting something straight, (3) and *instruction* refers to training, such as instructing a child. What is the end result of being a doer of the Word and not just a hearer (see verses 16–17)?

_____

_____

_____

_____

_____

_____

The Gospels reveal that Jesus likewise placed a high value on the need to not only *know* God's Word but also to *apply* it to the situations of life. The story of Jesus' temptation in the wilderness offers a master class in how to apply God's Word to the choices we make. Jesus bested Satan by holding fast to God's truth in the face of distortions and lies.

Satan Tempts Jesus (Matthew 4:1–4)

 ¹ Then Jesus was led up by the Spirit into the wilderness to be tempted by the devil. ² And when He had fasted forty days and forty nights, afterward He was hungry. ³ Now when the tempter came to Him, he said, "If You are the Son of God, command that these stones become bread."

⁴ But He answered and said, "It is written, 'Man shall not live by bread alone, but by every word that proceeds from the mouth of God.' "

7. The Holy Spirit led Jesus into the wilderness right after His baptism, where He fasted for forty days and nights. How did Satan take advantage of this situation (see verses 1–3)?

8. Jesus responded to Satan's first temptation by quoting a passage from the Old Testament: "Man shall not live by bread alone; but man lives by every word that proceeds from the mouth of the LORD" (Deuteronomy 8:3). How does this response from Christ demonstrate the power of God's Word in our lives (see verse 4)?

_____

_____

_____

_____

_____

REVIEWING THE STORY

James urges his readers to not just be *hearers* of God's Word but actual *doers* of God's Word. He uses the analogy of a man who looks into a mirror and immediately forgets what he looks like to show the difference between the two extremes. He adds that the one who chooses to investigate the "perfect law of liberty" and acts on it will be blessed in what he or she does. James concludes with a few examples of what being a doer looks like—controlling the tongue, helping orphans and widows, and keeping oneself unspotted from the world.

9. What is the implanted Word of God able to do (see James 1:21)?

_____

_____

_____

_____

_____

_____

10. How do people deceive themselves when it comes to God's Word (see James 1:22)?

_____

_____

_____

_____

_____

11. How are mere hearers of the word similar to the man who looked into a mirror and immediately forget what he looked like (see James 1:23–25)?

_____

_____

_____

_____

_____

12. What does James say is the difference between "useless" religion and "pure and undefiled" religion (see James 1:26–27)?

_____

_____

_____

_____

_____

APPLYING THE MESSAGE

13. What steps are you taking to be a hearer of the Word—to know what the Bible says?

_____

_____

_____

_____

_____

_____

_____

_____

14. What steps are you taking to be a doer of the Word—to put that knowledge into practice?

_____

_____

_____

_____

_____

_____

_____

_____

_____

REFLECTING ON THE MEANING

James concludes the opening chapter of his letter with a call for believers in Christ to approach God's Word with the proper attitude. However, true to form, James does not leave us with just that command. Instead, he outlines five practical steps that we can take to make sure that we are actively applying God's truths to our lives—allowing those truths to shape our actions.

First, we must hear the Word (see verse 19). We must focus our attention on what the Bible is actually saying. After all, before we can act on God's Word, we have to have an understanding of what it says. This means making it a priority to spend time in Scripture, investigating what it is saying to us, and asking the Lord for clarity and discernment.

Second, we must receive the Word (see verse 21). We should actively desire God's Word. If this reaction does not happen naturally, we can seek God's assistance by praying, "Lord, I long to hear what You have to say to me. Please teach me what You want me to know."

Third, we must apply the Word. James instructs, "Be doers of the word, and not hearers only, deceiving yourselves" (verse 22). Those who take a casual approach to studying God's Word allow its teachings to pass through their eyes or ears without a second thought. They refuse to consider God's Word because they don't want to face the truth it reveals about their lives. However, those who take a careful approach intently examine the truth and meaning of the Word. They desire to put into practice everything that God is saying.

Fourth, we must meditate on the Word (see verse 25). James urges us to continue in God's Word. Its truth should be constantly present in our thoughts. Meditating on the Word of God is the key to success, prosperity, and blessing (see Joshua 1:8 and Psalm 1:1–2).

Fifth, we must demonstrate the Word (see verses 26–27). If we take God's Word seriously, we will exhibit self-control, show compassion for those in need, and avoid corruption. We will conduct our lives in such a way that we will not be ashamed to one day face our Lord.

JOURNALING YOUR RESPONSE

Which of these steps is the most difficult for you? Why is it so difficult?

DANGEROUS FAVORITISM

James 2:1–7

GETTING STARTED

What are some of the causes of division that you see in the church today?

_____

_____

_____

_____

_____

_____

_____

_____

_____

_____

_____

_____

_____

_____

SETTING THE STAGE

We live in a world divided into two groups: *us* and *them*. We assign these categories based on the most superficial of reasons: *appearance, age, politics.*

We allow our differences to influence our attitudes. The love we are supposed to have for our neighbors becomes conditional. We surround ourselves with those who are like us and shy away from those who are not. We grow comfortable with embracing the qualities that separate us.

As a result, we tend to lose empathy for "them." We carve out an echo chamber for ourselves in which only the voices of "us" are heard and encouraged. Left unchecked, our attitude curdles into favoritism, prejudice, and injustice. We begin to identify ourselves not by the One we serve, but by those whom we oppose.

Obviously, such lack of unity should not exist in the body of Christ, where oneness is essential. But unfortunately, those divisions exist. Furthermore, this problem is not unique to our modern times but was prevalent during the days of the early church. As James reveals in this next section of his letter, the prejudices and preferential treatment occurring among the early Christians was seriously undermining the church's ministry and witness. The problem was so widespread that James decided to devote an entire section of his letter to it.

His particular focus is discrimination based on *wealth*. Quite simply, the rich people were being given preferential treatment in churches while the poor people were being pushed aside and ignored. The roots of this discrimination ran deep in the culture—and the effects it caused were devastating. But James's words have even broader application for us today. They challenge us to examine our hearts to see if we are harboring any prejudice of our own.

EXPLORING THE TEXT

Beware of Personal Favoritism (James 2:1–4)

¹ My brethren, do not hold the faith of our Lord Jesus Christ, the Lord of glory, with partiality. ² For if there should come into your assembly a man with gold rings, in fine apparel, and there should also come in a poor man in filthy clothes, ³ and you pay attention

to the one wearing the fine clothes and say to him, "You sit here in a good place," and say to the poor man, "You stand there," or, "Sit here at my footstool," [4] have you not shown partiality among yourselves, and become judges with evil thoughts?

1. The phrase *hold the faith* refers to a public posture of identifying oneself as a follower of Christ. What kind of attitude is incompatible with holding the faith (see verse 1)?

2. James offers a hypothetical situation of a rich man entering a congregation, but it is one that would have been recognizable to his readers. What happens when God's people allow appearances to dictate the way they treat visitors to the church (see verses 2–4)?

Rich in Faith (James 2:5–7)

[5] Listen, my beloved brethren: Has God not chosen the poor of this world to be rich in faith and heirs of the kingdom which He promised to those who love Him? [6] But you have dishonored the poor man. Do not the rich oppress you and drag you into the courts? [7] Do they not blaspheme that noble name by which you are called?

3. Poverty and piety are closely linked in the Old Testament and in ancient Jewish literature, perhaps because the poor are more likely to recognize their need for God. How does James say their heavenly position contrasts with their earthly position (see verses 5–6)?

_____

_____

_____

_____

4. In the first-century Roman world, wealthy landowners took advantage of the poor by forcing those individuals to work for them. In what other ways did these landowners show themselves to be unworthy of honor or special treatment (see verses 6–7)?

_____

_____

_____

_____

GOING DEEPER

When we consider that the first-century church was comprised of people from different ethnicities, with different social and economic standings, and from different backgrounds, it is little wonder that division was so prevalent. But the authors of the New Testament also knew how dangerous these divisions could be to the health and mission of the church. In the following passage, Paul emphasizes the importance of unity and urges believers to adopt a new mindset toward their fellow brothers and sisters in the faith—regardless of their differences.

Walk in Unity (Ephesians 4:1–6)

[1] I, therefore, the prisoner of the Lord, beseech you to walk worthy of the calling with which you were called, [2] with all lowliness and gentleness, with longsuffering, bearing with one another in love, [3] endeavoring to keep the unity of the Spirit in the bond of peace. [4] There is one body and one Spirit, just as you were called in one hope of your calling; [5] one Lord, one faith, one baptism; [6] one God and Father of all, who is above all, and through all, and in you all.

5. *Bearing with* means "to put up with." How does having an attitude of lowliness and gentleness help us put up with other believers (see verses 1–3)?

_____

_____

_____

_____

_____

_____

6. The word *endeavoring* means "to make every effort." What reminder does Paul offer to help us do the difficult work of treating people fairly in the church (see verses 3–6)?

_____

_____

_____

_____

_____

Paul also explored the theme of unity in the body of Christ in his letter to the Galatians. In doing so, he shines a spotlight on the categories we use to draw distinctions between us and others—distinctions that can get in the way of our unity and cause us to treat one another unfairly.

Sons and Heirs (Galatians 3:26–29)

> [26] For you are all sons of God through faith in Christ Jesus. [27] For as many of you as were baptized into Christ have put on Christ. [28] There is neither Jew nor Greek, there is neither slave nor free, there is neither male nor female; for you are all one in Christ Jesus. [29] And if you are Christ's, then you are Abraham's seed, and heirs according to the promise.

7. Paul stresses that all believers have been adopted by God and are members of his family. What does God's adopted family look like (see verses 26–28)?

_____

_____

_____

_____

8. Racial, social, and gender distinctions mean nothing to Christ. What is it that believers share in common that supersedes these distinctions (see verses 27–29)?

_____

_____

_____

_____

_____

_____

REVIEWING THE STORY

The early church was comprised of a diverse group of people. The wealthy, powerful, and socially connected worshiped with the outcasts of society. Or, at least, that was how it should have been. In reality, the people of the church were showing favoritism to the wealthy and mistreating the poor. In doing so, they were upending God's system, for He extends special favor to the poor. The people in the church were also rewarding bad behavior, for the rich people they honored were guilty of oppressing the poor and blaspheming God's name.

9. What attitude does James warn believers to avoid (see James 2:1)?

_____

_____

_____

_____

10. What happens when believers show partiality (see James 2:4)?

_____

_____

_____

11. Why did the believers' dishonoring of the poor displease God (see James 2:5–6)?

_____

_____

_____

_____

12. Why were the believers working against their own interests by honoring the wealthy (see James 2:6–7)?

_____

_____

_____

_____

APPLYING THE MESSAGE

13. What evidence of partiality do you see in your own life?

_____

_____

_____

14. What steps could you take to change this attitude?

_____

_____

_____

REFLECTING ON THE MEANING

In Acts 10, we read how Peter received a vision in which God showed him all kinds of animals. The Lord told him to "kill and eat," which caused Peter to protest, "Not so, Lord! For I have never eaten anything common or unclean." God replied to Peter, "What God has cleansed you must not call common" (verses 13–15). Peter got the message: "God shows no partiality. But in every nation whoever fears Him and works righteousness is accepted by Him" (verses 34–35). Unfortunately, the church continued to struggle with this issue. So, James offered five reasons in chapter 2 of his letter as to why this kind of favoritism has no place in the life of a believer.

First, favoritism is incompatible with the Christian faith. The author's use of the word *partiality* in James 2:1 suggests that undue favoritism was being shown to the wealthier church visitors while little attention was being paid to the poorer ones. According to James, such conduct was dishonoring to the Lord, who is never a respecter of persons. There is no room among Christians for prejudice, hatred, or judgment. God only has one family, and if we are in Christ, we are all in that family with equal footing and status.

Second, favoritism is insensitive to the church's calling. James talks about a visitor to the church in verses 2–4 who doesn't know where to sit. However, because he appears to be wealthy, he is given the royal treatment and ushered to a prominent seat. A poor man who follows him is shoved to one side and treated with disdain. Instead of being caught up with the glory of the Lord, the members were caught up in the splendor of the rich man. Instead of honoring Jesus Christ, they were paying respect to the rich and despising the poor.

Third, favoritism is inconsiderate of God's choices. James emphasizes in verse 5 that God has a special place in His heart for the poor. So, when believers treat rich people with respect and poor people with disrespect, they are upside down with God's values.

Fourth, favoritism is illogical. James reminds his friends in verses 6–7 that they are showing special treatment to the people who were oppressing them, dragging them into court, and blaspheming God's name. They were enabling their own abuse because they were overawed by wealthy people or because they hoped to gain something from them.

Fifth, favoritism is ignorant of future judgment. James writes, "So speak and so do as those who will be judged by the law of liberty. For judgment is without mercy to the one who has shown no mercy. Mercy triumphs over judgment. Mercy triumphs over judgment" (verses 12–13). The point James is making is that if we show mercy to others in our speech and in our actions, we will triumph at the judgment seat of Christ. As people who have been truly changed by the grace of God, we should no longer see others in class distinctions.

Journaling Your Response

How will you seek to better view others the way that God sees them?

A FAITH WITH INTEGRITY

James 2:8–17

GETTING STARTED

How have the good deeds of another believer in Christ impacted you personally in your life?

_____

_____

_____

_____

_____

_____

_____

_____

_____

_____

_____

_____

_____

_____

SETTING THE STAGE

Our society is trending toward *convenience*. Every innovation, it seems, is designed to reduce the amount of effort we expend. Don't want to push a cart through a grocery store? Order online and let someone deliver it to your home. Can't be bothered to parallel park? Take your hands off the wheel and let your automobile's automatic sensors do it for you. Tired of those long lines at theme parks? Invest in the express pass and skip the wait.

While the convenience of these innovations is enjoyable, the problem comes when we expect it in other areas of life. This is especially true in our spiritual life, where effortlessness is not only counterproductive but can also be dangerous. As a case in point, many people want to call themselves Christians without conforming to Christian truths or performing Christian acts. They want the immediate benefits of a relationship with God but without any disruptions to their routine, comfort, or resources. They want a personalized faith—one that elevates their preferences and fits nicely within their comfort zone.

We could attribute this personalized Christianity mindset to the inward-looking nature of our "selfie" culture. But the truth is this is not a new problem. In fact, it is more than 2,000 years old. In this next section of James, the author singles out certain individuals who were speaking the language of Christianity without reflecting the reality of its truth in their lives. They were all talk and no walk. James makes it clear that if we *say* we have faith in Christ, there needs to be *evidence* to back up our claim. Otherwise, what benefit is there to it?

James asks us to take a look at some of the spurious kinds of faith so that we might be better able to decide whether we have real faith. He invites us to pursue a faith with integrity. And this is the kind of faith that Jesus calls us to seek after as well.

EXPLORING THE TEXT

Follow the Royal Law (James 2:8–11)

⁸ If you really fulfill the royal law according to the Scripture, "You shall love your neighbor as yourself," you do well; ⁹ but if you show partiality, you commit sin, and are convicted by the law as transgressors.

[10] For whoever shall keep the whole law, and yet stumble in one point, he is guilty of all. [11] For He who said, "Do not commit adultery," also said, "Do not murder." Now if you do not commit adultery, but you do murder, you have become a transgressor of the law.

---

1. The "royal law" to which James refers is found Leviticus 19:18— "You shall love your neighbor as yourself." This law is *royal* because it represents the way that people are to love one another under the rule of our King. As believers, we are doing well if we are fulfilling this command. But what happens when we do not follow this law (see verses 8–9)?

_____

_____

_____

_____

_____

2. Many of us have a tendency to consider some sins to be greater than others, but James stresses there is no part of God's law that we can treat lightly. If we stumble on what we consider to be a minor point, we are still guilty of breaking God's law—and sinning. What examples does James use to emphasize this truth (see verses 10–11)?

_____

_____

_____

_____

_____

Faith Without Works Is Dead (James 2:12–17)

¹² So speak and so do as those who will be judged by the law of liberty. ¹³ For judgment is without mercy to the one who has shown no mercy. Mercy triumphs over judgment.

¹⁴ What does it profit, my brethren, if someone says he has faith but does not have works? Can faith save him? ¹⁵ If a brother or sister is naked and destitute of daily food, ¹⁶ and one of you says to them, "Depart in peace, be warmed and filled," but you do not give them the things which are needed for the body, what does it profit? ¹⁷ Thus also faith by itself, if it does not have works, is dead.

3. James notes that following God's law involves being merciful to others in both our speech and actions. As Jesus said, "Blessed are the merciful, for they shall obtain mercy" (Matthew 5:7). What is the warning if we fail to show God's mercy to others (see James 2:12–13)?

4. James states there is no *profit*—no benefit or advantage—if we say we have faith in Christ but do not live out the message of that gospel through our words and deeds. We have a *dead* faith that is so spiritually deficient that it calls into question its very reality. What hypothetical situation does James use to illustrate such a dead faith (see verses 14–17)?

_____

_____

_____

_____

_____

_____

_____

_____

GOING DEEPER

The primary contention that James makes in this section of his letter is that faith should be accompanied by good works in a believer's life. While good works can never save a person, they represent the outward evidence that the person's life is being transformed from within. Jesus likewise spoke of the "fruits" that will be produced in a person who is truly following Him.

Known by Their Fruits (Matthew 7:15–23)

15 "Beware of false prophets, who come to you in sheep's clothing, but inwardly they are ravenous wolves. 16 You will know them by their fruits. Do men gather grapes from thornbushes or figs from thistles? 17 Even so, every good tree bears good fruit, but a bad tree bears bad fruit. 18 A good tree cannot bear bad fruit, nor can a bad tree bear good fruit. 19 Every tree that does not bear good fruit is cut down and thrown into the fire. 20 Therefore by their fruits you will know them.

²¹ "Not everyone who says to Me, 'Lord, Lord,' shall enter the kingdom of heaven, but he who does the will of My Father in heaven. ²² Many will say to Me in that day, 'Lord, Lord, have we not prophesied in Your name, cast out demons in Your name, and done many wonders in Your name?' ²³ And then I will declare to them, 'I never knew you; depart from Me, you who practice lawlessness!'"

---

5. The word *fruits* refers not only to doctrines and teachings but also to a person's deeds. What does Jesus say about the "tree" from which fruit is produced? What is he saying about the state of a person's heart who does not desire to do good works (see verses 16–20)?

_____

_____

_____

_____

_____

_____

_____

6. Jesus' words in verses 21–23 deal not with false prophets but with false followers. What is Jesus saying here about the importance of not just *saying* but actually *doing* God's will?

_____

_____

_____

_____

_____

Other authors of the New Testament also draw a connection between faith and good works in a believers' life. In his first letter, the apostle John asks a pointed question about those who refuse to put their faith into action. Like James, he places a special emphasis on not merely giving lip service to our Christian love but actually acting on our faith.

The Outworking of Love (1 John 3:16–23)

16 By this we know love, because He laid down His life for us. And we also ought to lay down our lives for the brethren. 17 But whoever has this world's goods, and sees his brother in need, and shuts up his heart from him, how does the love of God abide in him?

18 My little children, let us not love in word or in tongue, but in deed and in truth. 19 And by this we know that we are of the truth, and shall assure our hearts before Him. 20 For if our heart condemns us, God is greater than our heart, and knows all things.

7. The word *goods* in verse 17 refers to the material objects that sustain life—items such as food, clothing, and shelter. How can we use these things to show others that the love of God abides within us (see verses 16–17)?

_____

_____

_____

_____

_____

_____

_____

_____

_____

_____

8. The phrase *love in word* (verse 18) means to speak loving words to others but to stop short of actually doing anything to demonstrate that love. What happens when we go beyond words and love others with our actions (see verses 18–20)?

_____

_____

_____

_____

_____

_____

REVIEWING THE STORY

James helps his readers recognize that showing partiality to others violates God's command to "love your neighbor as yourself" (Leviticus 19:18). This is not a minor infraction that can be dismissed but a violation of the entire law. Furthermore, those who do not show mercy cannot expect to receive mercy themselves. James continues by issuing a warning to those who claim to put their faith in Christ but do not demonstrate an outward expression of their changed life. True faith must always lead to action—otherwise, it is a dead faith, useless to everyone.

9. How do we know if we're doing well in following the "royal law" of God (see James 2:8)?

_____

_____

_____

_____

_____

_____

10. Why is it so important that our actions align with our words (see James 2:12)?

_____

_____

_____

_____

_____

_____

_____

11. How should believers _not_ respond to someone who is truly in need (see James 2:15–16)?

_____

_____

_____

_____

_____

_____

_____

_____

12. What keeps faith alive (see James 2:17)?

_____

_____

_____

_____

_____

_____

_____

APPLYING THE MESSAGE

13. How have you seen God actively reach out to extend mercy to you?

_____

_____

_____

_____

_____

14. What are some ways you are acting on your faith and genuinely loving and serving others?

_____

_____

_____

_____

_____

REFLECTING ON THE MEANING

When Jesus was teaching the people one day, He said to them, "The scribes and the Pharisees sit in Moses' seat. Therefore whatever they tell you to observe, that observe and do, but do not do according to their works; for they say, and do not do" (Matthew 23:2–3). Jesus was referring to the religious leaders of the day, and He did not mince words in calling out their hypocrisy. They were claiming they were righteous . . . but there was no evidence of this in their lives.

We find James emphasizing this same principle in this section of his letter. But this time, the words are aimed at those who claim to be followers of Christ. For James, true Christian faith involves more than just a verbal affirmation. If we have truly been born anew, our lives will reflect that new birth. In the words of Paul, "If anyone is in Christ, he is a new creation; old things have passed away; behold, all things have become new" (2 Corinthians 5:17). James goes on to provide several reasons as to why a verbal faith alone is not sufficient for a believer.

First, a verbal faith alone does not save. James uses two rhetorical questions in verse 14: "What does it profit, my brethren, if someone says he has faith but does not have works? Can faith save him?" In other words, a faith that does not demonstrate its genuineness in works is not genuine. Now, it is important to note that James is not implying good works are *required* for salvation. After all, Paul says we are saved by faith alone (see Ephesians 2:8). However, we do not become Christians just by *saying* we are Christians. True Christianity goes much deeper than the mere affirmation of the tongue. It requires a change in our lives.

Second, a verbal faith alone does not serve. James uses a stirring illustration in verses 15–16 to drive home this point. He asks his readers to imagine a person who shows up at the door of a believer asking for help. But instead of helping the needy person, the Christian says, "Depart in peace, be warmed and filled." He doesn't give him the things he needs. This professing Christian, according to James, has cast doubt upon the integrity of his own faith.

How often do we do this? How many times does somebody come to us with a real need and we just say a prayer for them and send them away? In such a situation, we should forget the prayer and just do what needs to be done. Instead of asking *God* to help them, *we* must be the ones to help them—an answer to our own prayer. After all, this may be why God sent them to us in the first place. If our faith isn't expressed in our daily life, it may not be genuine.

Third, a verbal faith alone does not survive. James says in verse 17 that faith unaccompanied by works "is dead." The lack of any fruit in the person's life is proof of a profession-only faith. James is pleading for reality in Christianity. He is not trying to add works to faith as a way to be saved but is just saying that if we have genuinely been saved, it will change our entire outlook. Our lives will be changed . . . and good works will be the result.

Journaling Your Response

How can you be the answer to your own prayer today for someone who is in need?

TAKE ACTION!

James 2:18–26

GETTING STARTED

What is the boldest thing that you have ever done for Christ?

_____

_____

_____

_____

_____

_____

_____

_____

_____

_____

_____

_____

SETTING THE STAGE

Many years ago, a man named Charles Blondin gained notoriety by performing dangerous stunts. Blondin was a tightrope walker, and perhaps his most unforgettable set of performances was walking across the mighty

Niagara Falls. Blondin did some amazing things on that wire. He walked across blindfolded. He pushed a wheelbarrow across and back. He even somersaulted and backflipped his way across, occasionally pausing to dangle from the cable by one hand.

The story is told that one day after Blondin crossed with a wheelbarrow, he asked the audience if they believed he could do it again. They cheered wildly to indicate their absolute confidence in him. Then he asked, "Could I have a volunteer to ride in the wheelbarrow?" Suddenly, the cheering stopped. After all, it's one thing to believe a person *can* do something . . . but it's another thing to believe *in* them to do something for you.

This is the point that James makes in this next section of his letter. Putting our faith in Christ requires more of us than merely believing in our head that Jesus is who He says He is. It requires us to believe Jesus will forgive our sins and do what He has promised He will do. It involves more than just having an optimistic outlook on life or feeling confident about eternity. Putting our faith in Jesus means living in a way that pleases Him, even when it takes us out of our comfort zone. It changes our outlook, priorities, decision-making, and relationships.

Furthermore, our faith in Christ isn't something that should go unnoticed. People should recognize the difference that He makes in our lives—based on our *actions*. There is a vast difference between mental assent and real faith. James explores this difference as he continues to encourage believers not to settle for just a verbal faith.

EXPLORING THE TEXT

Faith Made Perfect (James 2:18–22)

¹⁸ But someone will say, "You have faith, and I have works." Show me your faith without your works, and I will show you my faith by my works. ¹⁹ You believe that there is one God. You do well. Even the demons believe—and tremble! ²⁰ But do you want to know, O foolish man, that faith without works is dead? ²¹ Was not Abraham

our father justified by works when he offered Isaac his son on the altar? [22] Do you see that faith was working together with his works, and by works faith was made perfect?

_____

1. James stresses that faith and works *always* go together—that works of righteousness are the expression of true faith. It is not enough to just have a head knowledge of God or recognize His reality. What example does he use to make this point (see verses 18–19)?

_____

_____

_____

_____

_____

_____

2. Paul often used the term *justified* to refer to a person's right standing before God based on Jesus' sacrifice on the cross (see Romans 3:24). But James uses the term *justified* in this passage to refer to God affirming a person based on his or her righteous actions. He draws on the story of Abraham offering Isaac as a sacrifice to reinforce his point (see Genesis 22). How did Abraham's actions bring his faith and works together (see James 2:20–22)?

_____

_____

_____

_____

_____

_____

Accounted as Righteousness (James 2:23–26)

²³ And the Scripture was fulfilled which says, "Abraham believed God, and it was accounted to him for righteousness." And he was called the friend of God. ²⁴ You see then that a man is justified by works, and not by faith only.

²⁵ Likewise, was not Rahab the harlot also justified by works when she received the messengers and sent them out another way?

²⁶ For as the body without the spirit is dead, so faith without works is dead also.

---

3. Abraham actively demonstrated his faith in God through his willingness to sacrifice Isaac—the son whom decades before God had promised to him—and the Lord credited it to him as righteousness (see Genesis 15:6). What conclusion does James make based on this story about the relationship between faith and works (see James 2:23–24)?

_____

_____

_____

_____

_____

_____

_____

4. James offers a second Old Testament story to reinforce his theme. Rahab professed her faith in God when she said to the spies, "The LORD your God, He is God in heaven above and on earth beneath" (Joshua 2:11). How did she then act on this faith? What conclusion

does James reach about faith and works based on her story
(see James 2:25–26)?

_____

_____

_____

_____

_____

_____

GOING DEEPER

James draws on the stories of two individuals from the Old Testament, both of whom would have been familiar to his readers, to make his point about the importance of acting on our faith. The first example, drawn from Genesis 22, recounts how Abraham acted on his faith in God by willingly offering Isaac as a sacrifice. The second illustration, drawn from Joshua 2, relates how Rahab acted on her faith in the God of Israel by harboring the spies—at the risk of her own life.

Abraham's Faith Confirmed (Genesis 22:1–12)

¹ Now it came to pass after these things that God tested Abraham, and said to him, "Abraham!"

And he said, "Here I am."

² Then He said, "Take now your son, your only son Isaac, whom you love, and go to the land of Moriah, and offer him there as a burnt offering on one of the mountains of which I shall tell you."

³ So Abraham rose early in the morning and saddled his donkey, and took two of his young men with him, and Isaac his son; and he split the wood for the burnt offering, and arose and went to the place of which God had told him. ⁴ Then on the third day Abraham lifted his eyes and saw the place afar off. ⁵ And Abraham said to his

young men, "Stay here with the donkey; the lad and I will go yonder and worship, and we will come back to you."

⁶ So Abraham took the wood of the burnt offering and laid it on Isaac his son; and he took the fire in his hand, and a knife, and the two of them went together. ⁷ But Isaac spoke to Abraham his father and said, "My father!"

And he said, "Here I am, my son."

Then he said, "Look, the fire and the wood, but where is the lamb for a burnt offering?"

⁸ And Abraham said, "My son, God will provide for Himself the lamb for a burnt offering." So the two of them went together.

⁹ Then they came to the place of which God had told him. And Abraham built an altar there and placed the wood in order; and he bound Isaac his son and laid him on the altar, upon the wood. ¹⁰ And Abraham stretched out his hand and took the knife to slay his son.

¹¹ But the Angel of the Lᴏʀᴅ called to him from heaven and said, "Abraham, Abraham!"

So he said, "Here I am."

¹² And He said, "Do not lay your hand on the lad, or do anything to him; for now I know that you fear God, since you have not withheld your son, your only son, from Me."

---

5. What was the test that God set before Abraham? How did Abraham respond when he received these instructions from the Lord (see verses 1–5)?

_____

_____

_____

_____

_____

6. What did God say and do when He saw that Abraham was willing to act on his faith and obediently offer his son Isaac as a sacrifice (see verses 9–12)?

_____

_____

_____

_____

_____

_____

Rahab Hides the Spies (Joshua 2:3–14)

³ So the king of Jericho sent to Rahab, saying, "Bring out the men who have come to you, who have entered your house, for they have come to search out all the country."

⁴ Then the woman took the two men and hid them. So she said, "Yes, the men came to me, but I did not know where they were from. ⁵ And it happened as the gate was being shut, when it was dark, that the men went out. Where the men went I do not know; pursue them quickly, for you may overtake them." ⁶ (But she had brought them up to the roof and hidden them with the stalks of flax, which she had laid in order on the roof.) ⁷ Then the men pursued them by the road to the Jordan, to the fords. And as soon as those who pursued them had gone out, they shut the gate.

⁸ Now before they lay down, she came up to them on the roof, ⁹ and said to the men: "I know that the LORD has given you the land, that the terror of you has fallen on us, and that all the inhabitants of the land are fainthearted because of you. ¹⁰ For we have heard how the LORD dried up the water of the Red Sea for you when you came out of Egypt, and what you did to the two kings of the Amorites who were on the other side of the Jordan, Sihon and Og, whom you utterly destroyed. ¹¹ And as soon as we heard these things, our

hearts melted; neither did there remain any more courage in anyone because of you, for the LORD your God, He is God in heaven above and on earth beneath. ¹² Now therefore, I beg you, swear to me by the LORD , since I have shown you kindness, that you also will show kindness to my father's house, and give me a true token, ¹³ and spare my father, my mother, my brothers, my sisters, and all that they have, and deliver our lives from death."

¹⁴ So the men answered her, "Our lives for yours, if none of you tell this business of ours. And it shall be, when the LORD has given us the land, that we will deal kindly and truly with you."

---

7. How did Rahab respond to the king of Jericho when he asked about the Israelite spies? Why was she willing to take this action (see verses 3–9)?

_____

_____

_____

_____

_____

8. What did Rahab say to the spies that reveals she feared the God of the Israelites? What request did she make for herself and her family (see verses 10–14)?

_____

_____

_____

_____

_____

_____

REVIEWING THE STORY

James helps believers understand there is no comparison between faith without works and faith with works. Faith without works is not a real, living, and active faith. Having a faith that meets the barest minimum of standards does not change us or set us apart in any way. After all, even the demons believe there is one God! The kind of faith we must strive to possess is the kind of faith demonstrated by both Abraham and Rahab. They did not just *profess* to believe in God. They both took unimaginable risks to *act* in obedience to Him.

9. What does James say to those who claim to have faith without works (see James 2:18)?

_____

_____

_____

_____

_____

_____

10. What do even the demons believe—and how do they react (see James 2:19)?

_____

_____

_____

_____

_____

_____

_____

11. How was Abraham justified by works (see James 2:21–22)?

_____

_____

_____

_____

_____

12. What analogy does James use to show the uselessness of faith without works (see James 2:26)?

_____

_____

_____

_____

APPLYING THE MESSAGE

13. What are some lessons you learned about faith from the stories of Abraham and Rahab?

_____

_____

_____

_____

_____

14. What are some bold risks that God has asked you to take?

_____

_____

_____

_____

_____

REFLECTING ON THE MEANING

James continues to make the case that faith without action is useless. Many people define faith as just a positive mental attitude. But James reveals that faith is more than an attitude. Faith is an *action*. James tells us that faith is made perfect by works—that we mature spiritually as we act in faith. His references to Abraham and Rahab drive his point home.

When God told Abraham to take Isaac—the son of promise—to Mount Moriah and there sacrifice him on an altar, we find that Abraham immediately acted on God's command and obeyed. "Abraham rose early in the morning and saddled his donkey, and took two of his young men with him, and Isaac his son; and he split the wood for the burnt offering, and arose and went to the place of which God had told him" (Genesis 22:3). If Abraham had said, "I believe God," but refused to obey, he would have had mental-assent faith—and not real faith. It was his trip to the mountain and his willingness to go through with the sacrifice that made the difference.

Likewise, in the story of Rahab protecting the Israelite spies, she was willing to defy the king of Jericho in order to act on her faith in God. She not only professed, "the LORD your God, He is God in heaven above and on earth beneath" (Joshua 2:11), but was also willing to put her life on the line to protect those representatives of God. This is why we find her name in the "Hall of Faith" in Hebrews 11. Rahab's works were different from Abraham's, but they had the same effect. They proved that she had a living, active, and working faith in God. Her story affirms James's contention that faith in Christ leads us to act differently.

We cannot just say, "I said some words to God a long time ago, so I'm a Christian, but basically nothing has changed in my life." The Bible says the same God who called us to salvation has called us to good works. We are not saved *by* works, but we are saved *for* works. Our faith produces good works that demonstrate Christ's unique work in our hearts—and with Christ in our hearts, we become visible beacons of His love, service, and compassion to others.

JOURNALING YOUR RESPONSE

What does it mean for you to be a visible beacon of Christ's love, service, and compassion?

WATCH YOUR WORDS

James 3:1–12

GETTING STARTED

When was the last time your words got you in trouble? What happened as a result?

_____

_____

_____

_____

_____

_____

_____

_____

_____

_____

_____

_____

_____

SETTING THE STAGE

Given the strident points that James makes in his letter, one would assume that he is talking to non-believers. But he is not. The word *brother* or *brethren* is found nineteen times in the book of James. He is addressing people who are members of the community of Christ. James continually reminds them that they are "brothers"—that they are part of the same family—and they need to start acting like it. This includes controlling their tongues.

It is incredible the kind of trouble that our tongues can create for us. This little bit of muscle can start wars and stop them. It can create stress and relieve it. It can express love and renounce it. It can build up friendships and then tear them down again. With our tongues we can praise and worship God, and with those same instruments we can curse God and deny His existence. As Scripture states, "Death and life are in the power of the tongue" (Proverbs 18:21).

The real issue at stake—the one James targets in this next section of his letter—is our ability or our inability to control our tongues. In fact, many of the biblical characters we revere had issues with their words. Moses became angry when the Israelites rebelled against God and "spoke rashly with his lips" (Psalm 106:33). Isaiah confessed that he was "a man of unclean lips" (Isaiah 6:5). Job admitted to God, "I have uttered what I did not understand" (Job 42:3).

We are not much different from these biblical figures. At times, each of us could admit to speaking rashly, or improperly, or ignorantly. We have to continually be careful of what we say and how we use the gift of speech that God has given us. This can be difficult, as James reminds us in this next section, but the truth is we *can* learn to manage our mouths.

EXPLORING THE TEXT

The Untamable Tongue (James 3:1–4)

¹ My brethren, let not many of you become teachers, knowing that we shall receive a stricter judgment. ² For we all stumble in many things. If anyone does not stumble in word, he is a perfect man, able also to bridle the whole body. ³ Indeed, we put bits in horses' mouths

that they may obey us, and we turn their whole body. [4] Look also at ships: although they are so large and are driven by fierce winds, they are turned by a very small rudder wherever the pilot desires.

1. James has made several references up to this point on the impact of our speech. He now reinforces his message using illustrations to address the issue of bickering and verbal strife occurring in the Christian community. He begins with the power that words have when they come from a teacher. Teachers had an exalted status in the early church, which led to many unfit people pursuing the position. What advice does James offer them (see verses 1–2)?

_____

_____

_____

_____

_____

_____

2. James points out that the tongue has incredible power even though it is only a small muscle in the body. How do the analogies of the horse's bit and ship's rudder illustrate this idea? What is James saying about the impact of our words (see verses 3–4)?

_____

_____

_____

_____

_____

_____

The Fiery Tongue (James 3:5–12)

[5] Even so the tongue is a little member and boasts great things. See how great a forest a little fire kindles! [6] And the tongue is a fire, a world of iniquity. The tongue is so set among our members that it defiles the whole body, and sets on fire the course of nature; and it is set on fire by hell. [7] For every kind of beast and bird, of reptile and creature of the sea, is tamed and has been tamed by mankind. [8] But no man can tame the tongue. It is an unruly evil, full of deadly poison. [9] With it we bless our God and Father, and with it we curse men, who have been made in the similitude of God. [10] Out of the same mouth proceed blessing and cursing. My brethren, these things ought not to be so. [11] Does a spring send forth fresh water and bitter from the same opening? [12] Can a fig tree, my brethren, bear olives, or a grapevine bear figs? Thus no spring yields both salt water and fresh.

3. The third analogy of the tongue as a wildfire emphasizes the destructive capabilities that our speech can have on ourselves and on others. The phrase *world of iniquity* suggests the tongue can actually serve as a representative of the enemy. All kinds of unrighteousness can be brought to life by the tongue. What are the results of this evil work (see verses 5–6)?

_____

_____

_____

_____

_____

_____

_____

_____

_____

_____

4. As we have seen, James took issue with believers who claimed to be loving others but whose lives did not reflect that love through acts of grace, mercy, and service. What does James say here about the "dual nature" of these believers as it relates to their speech? What point is he making through the spring and fig tree illustrations (see verses 9–12)?

_____

_____

_____

_____

_____

_____

_____

_____

_____

GOING DEEPER

The epistle of James is widely considered to be New Testament "wisdom literature," in that it is comprised of moral exhortations and calls for believers to act on the wisdom that God has provided. James echoes many of the words that Jesus spoke in the Gospels. However, as the following passage reveals, he also echoed words of wisdom given in the Old Testament.

Honor Is Not Fitting for a Fool (Proverbs 26:18–22)

[18] Like a madman who throws firebrands, arrows, and death,
[19] Is the man who deceives his neighbor,
And says, "I was only joking!"

[20] Where there is no wood, the fire goes out;
And where there is no talebearer, strife ceases.

²¹ As charcoal is to burning coals, and wood to fire,

So is a contentious man to kindle strife.

²² The words of a talebearer are like tasty trifles,

And they go down into the inmost body.

---

5. The writer's use of the violent imagery "firebrands, arrows, and death" suggests that the damage done by a deceitful tongue cannot always be undone (see verses 18–19). How does this agree or disagree with what James said about the power of the tongue?

6. The word *talebearer* refers to someone who spreads rumors and gossip. What effects do the words of a talebearer have on a community (see verses 20–22)?

Of course, the problem of believers controlling their tongues was not limited to only the communities that James was addressing. Paul was also keenly aware of the destruction and disunity an unbridled tongue could bring. In the following passage, he gives Timothy some advice to help his congregation understand the power of their words.

Wholesome Speech (1 Timothy 6:3–5)

³ If anyone teaches otherwise and does not consent to wholesome words, even the words of our Lord Jesus Christ, and to the doctrine which accords with godliness, ⁴ he is proud, knowing nothing, but is obsessed with disputes and arguments over words, from which come envy, strife, reviling, evil suspicions, ⁵ useless wranglings of men of corrupt minds and destitute of the truth, who suppose that godliness is a means of gain. From such withdraw yourself.

7. The phrase *wholesome words* that Paul employs refers to the sound instruction the believers had received from him and other godly teachers—and the words of Christ. What does Paul say about the person who rejects this sound doctrine (see verses 3–4)?

_____

_____

_____

_____

_____

_____

_____

_____

8. Paul's use of the words *disputes* and *arguments* refers to any irrelevant issues that sidetrack the outworking of people's faith. What happens when such irrelevant issues are allowed to take center stage (see verses 4–5)?

_____

_____

_____

_____

_____

_____

_____

Reviewing the Story

James singles out the tongue as a key to living a life that pleases God. If we can master it, then we can master our entire body. He compares the power and usefulness of the tongue to a bit in a horse's mouth and the rudder of a large ship, noting that in spite of the tongue being a small member of the body, it has great power over us. James also compares the tongue to a flame that is capable of doing great damage. He warns us about how difficult it is to tame, and adds that the same mouth used to bless God should never be used to curse others.

9. What happens when we learn to control our tongue (see James 3:2)?

_____

_____

_____

_____

_____

_____

10. What are some of the positive things that our words can do (see James 3:3–4)?

_____

_____

_____

_____

_____

_____

_____

11. What potential for destruction is contained in our tongues (see James 3:6–8)?

_____

_____

_____

_____

_____

_____

_____

12. What is the warning to those who both praise God and curse others (see James 3:9–12)?

_____

_____

_____

_____

_____

_____

_____

APPLYING THE MESSAGE

13. What is your biggest challenge that you have when it comes to controlling your words?

_____

_____

_____

_____

_____

_____

_____

_____

_____

14. What specific steps can you take to rise to that challenge?

_____

_____

_____

_____

_____

_____

_____

_____

_____

_____

_____

REFLECTING ON THE MEANING

Up to this point, James has been stressing the importance for believers in Christ to back up their words with godly *actions*. However, as he moves into chapter 3, he is careful to note that our *words*—and how we use them—are also vitally important. James emphasizes this point by stressing two key areas in which we must be especially cautious in using our words.

First, we must be cautious when instructing others. James writes, "My brethren, let not many of you become teachers, knowing that we shall receive a stricter judgment" (3:1). James stresses that teaching is not a pursuit to be taken lightly. Teachers can—and *do*—use the power of their tongues to influence many people. This can result in a heady experience for them, especially if they are not fully grounded in God's truth.

We all know that teachers can have a powerful influence. Just consider some of the teachers you had growing up—gifted instructors who not only gave you knowledge but who also mentored you as an individual. These teachers understood that with the power to shape lives comes great responsibility. As Jesus taught in Luke 12:48, "For everyone to whom much is given, from him much will be required." Teachers of the Word are held to even higher standards, for they have the power to provide the very words of life and death to others.

Second, we must be cautious when interacting with others. James writes, "For we all stumble in many things. If anyone does not stumble in word, he is a perfect man, able also to bridle the whole body" (verse 2). In other words, if we can learn to control our tongues, then we will not have any trouble in controlling the rest of ourselves. The control of the tongue is the most difficult assignment that we will ever have.

One mark of Christian maturity is control of the tongue. All of us know people who may not say much, but when they do, we want to write down every word. When we are in their presence, they may not get involved in the give-and-take of the discussion. But after everyone else has worn themselves out talking, these people will say something of great value. This is the kind of maturity and restraint we need to have as Christians.

Mature Christians don't have to look back with regret at what they have said, because they have control of their tongues.

JOURNALING YOUR RESPONSE

How can you use your words today to bring wisdom and encouragement to another person?

WISDOM FROM ABOVE

James 3:13–18

GETTING STARTED

What steps do you go through to judge the wisest course of action in a given situation?

_____

_____

_____

_____

_____

_____

_____

_____

_____

_____

_____

_____

_____

_____

SETTING THE STAGE

The problem of putting trust in worldly wisdom has plagued humanity ever since Satan tempted Adam and Eve in the Garden of Eden. We like to believe that we can figure things out independent of any divine help. So, when something seems right to us—when it agrees with our understanding of the world around us—we declare it to be wisdom.

We see this play out in society every day. The business world tells us that if we want to be successful, we have to put aside our morals and pursue the almighty dollar at any cost. The social media world tells us that if we want people to like us, we have to post pictures of ourselves doing incredible things and earn as many "likes" as possible. And the world at large tells us that if we want to get anywhere in life, we must never admit our failures, show weakness of any kind, or let people see us for who we truly are.

All of this represents worldly wisdom that runs counter to the teachings in the Bible. God's wisdom, instead, reveals that "the love of money is a root of all kinds of evil" (1 Timothy 6:10) and that we should "seek first the kingdom of God" (Matthew 6:33). His wisdom states that whoever desires to become great in His sight must first become a servant of all (see Matthew 20:26). His wisdom shows us that "God has chosen the weak things of the world to put to shame the things which are mighty" (1 Corinthians 1:27).

In the end, we find that putting our faith in worldly wisdom is a risky proposition. This is the message that James wants to relate to his readers as he closes out this section of his letter. He exposes the dark underbelly of worldly wisdom and encourages us to consider carefully where we place our trust. James reminds us that the wisdom we need on which to build a solid life foundation comes from God alone. God's wisdom leads us to our Creator and enables us to see life from an eternal perspective.

EXPLORING THE TEXT

Wisdom and Works (James 3:13–14)

¹³ Who is wise and understanding among you? Let him show by good conduct that his works are done in the meekness of wisdom.

¹⁴ But if you have bitter envy and self-seeking in your hearts, do not boast and lie against the truth.

---

1. In the ancient world, to be *wise* meant to be knowledgeable or experienced in some area of life. However, James uses the term to refer to an understanding that comes from God, who is the source of all wisdom. It may be that some people in the churches were boasting of their learning. How does James say true wisdom speaks loudest (see verse 13)?

_____

_____

_____

_____

_____

_____

_____

2. The word *self-seeking* refers to those people in the church who were setting themselves over others and advancing their own agendas. What does James say that these individuals should *not* do in the church (see verse 14)?

_____

_____

_____

_____

_____

_____

_____

Heavenly Versus Demonic Wisdom (James 3:15–18)

---

[15] This wisdom does not descend from above, but is earthly, sensual, demonic. [16] For where envy and self-seeking exist, confusion and every evil thing are there. [17] But the wisdom that is from above is first pure, then peaceable, gentle, willing to yield, full of mercy and good fruits, without partiality and without hypocrisy. [18] Now the fruit of righteousness is sown in peace by those who make peace.

---

3. James is clear that the kind of wisdom that promotes bitter envy and self-seeking is not from God but is earthly in nature. In other words, such worldly wisdom is twisted and immoral. What will be the fruits of this kind of wisdom (see verses 15–16)?

_____

_____

_____

_____

_____

_____

4. The Greek phrase translated as "willing to yield" is a military term that means "to be willing to take instructions." How does such an attitude contribute to peace (see verses 17–18)?

_____

_____

_____

_____

_____

_____

GOING DEEPER

The letters of Paul also provide us with insights into the differences between earthly wisdom and godly wisdom. In his first letter to the Corinthians, the apostle comments on the nature of the "earthly" or "natural" man who doesn't understand the Holy Spirit's wisdom. In his letter to the Colossians, he gives us a snapshot of how godly wisdom should translate into godly actions.

Spiritual Wisdom (1 Corinthians 2:13–16)

¹³ These things we also speak, not in words which man's wisdom teaches but which the Holy Spirit teaches, comparing spiritual things with spiritual. ¹⁴ But the natural man does not receive the things of the Spirit of God, for they are foolishness to him; nor can he know them, because they are spiritually discerned. ¹⁵ But he who is spiritual judges all things, yet he himself is rightly judged by no one. ¹⁶ For "who has known the mind of the LORD that he may instruct Him?" But we have the mind of Christ.

5. Paul states that the natural man—the person who relies on worldly wisdom—does not receive the things of the Holy Spirit. The word *receive*, in this context, means to welcome. Why does the natural man reject God's wisdom (see verses 13–14)?

_____

_____

_____

_____

_____

_____

6. By contrast, the spiritual man—the person who has accepted the message of the gospel—has received the Holy Spirit. What does this allow that person to do (see verses 15–16)?

_____

_____

_____

_____

_____

_____

_____

_____

_____

_____

_____

Character of the New Man (Colossians 3:12–17)

[12] Therefore, as the elect of God, holy and beloved, put on tender mercies, kindness, humility, meekness, longsuffering; [13] bearing with one another, and forgiving one another, if anyone has a complaint against another; even as Christ forgave you, so you also must do. [14] But above all these things put on love, which is the bond of perfection. [15] And let the peace of God rule in your hearts, to which also you were called in one body; and be thankful. [16] Let the word of Christ dwell in you richly in all wisdom, teaching and admonishing one another in psalms and hymns and spiritual songs, singing with grace in your hearts to the Lord. [17] And whatever you do in word or deed, do all in the name of the Lord Jesus, giving thanks to God the Father through Him.

7. Paul uses three words to describe believers: *elect*, which means selected for His family; *holy*, which means set apart as a result of God's work; and *beloved*, which refers to the relationship we enjoy with God. How should our wisdom and knowledge concerning our spiritual identity affect our daily choices and interactions (see verses 12–15)?

_____

_____

_____

_____

_____

_____

_____

_____

8. The source of our wisdom is "the word of Christ," which refers to Christ's teachings—those found in the gospels and explained by the apostles. How does the indwelling of the word of Christ make itself known in our relationships with other believers (see verses 16–17)?

_____

_____

_____

_____

_____

_____

_____

_____

_____

REVIEWING THE STORY

James opens this section of his letter with a rhetorical question: "Who is wise and understanding among you?" (3:13). Those who are truly wise—who embrace heavenly wisdom—make their wisdom known through their actions. They don't brag about their learning and understanding. Instead, they let it guide their attitudes and decision-making. This heavenly wisdom stands in stark contrast to earthly wisdom, which inspires pride, envy, and self-centeredness. Earthly wisdom causes confusion and leads people astray, while heavenly wisdom yields the fruit of righteousness—which will be readily apparent to others.

9. How does godly wisdom make itself known (see James 3:13)?

_____

_____

_____

_____

_____

_____

_____

10. What are the fruits of earthly wisdom (see James 3:14)?

_____

_____

_____

_____

_____

_____

_____

_____

11. Where do does earthly wisdom ultimately lead (see James 3:16)?

_____

_____

_____

_____

_____

_____

12. What are the fruits of righteousness that come from godly wisdom (see James 3:17)?

_____

_____

_____

_____

_____

_____

APPLYING THE MESSAGE

13. What are some effective methods you have discovered for gaining spiritual wisdom?

_____

_____

_____

_____

_____

_____

14. What are some of the results you have experienced when you have operated out of earthly wisdom?

REFLECTING ON THE MEANING

If we are to be guided by heavenly wisdom, we need to understand what it is and how it works. James's description of godly wisdom in this section of his epistle is an excellent place to start. He writes, "The wisdom that is from above is first pure, then peaceable, gentle, willing to yield, full of mercy and good fruits, without partiality and without hypocrisy" (3:17). In this verse, James gives us the following seven characteristics of heavenly wisdom.

First, heavenly wisdom is pure. Purity is first on James's list because God's wisdom—like His nature—is based on His holiness. There are no hidden motives in God's wisdom; it is transparent and clean. There is nothing hidden under the surface; it is all up front.

Second, heavenly wisdom is peaceable. True peace is always the outgrowth of purity in our lives. Peace is a blessing that comes to us from God and is available to us from Him alone. Peace is a lighthouse in the midst of a raging storm. When we are going through a difficult time, God's presence is there. He promises to give us great and perfect peace (see Isaiah 26:3; Psalm 119:165).

Third, heavenly wisdom is gentle. Strife is the world's wisdom, but gentleness is a property of the wisdom from above.

Fourth, heavenly wisdom is willing to yield. God's wisdom has a conciliatory spirit and listens to reason. The Greek term translated by the phrase "willing to yield" is found only in this verse in the New Testament. It is a military term that means "to be willing to take instructions." When the spiritually wise are in command, they must be gentle. But when they are under authority, they must be willing to yield—to take instruction.

Fifth, heavenly wisdom is full of mercy and good fruits. Our wisdom is demonstrated by our behavior. Our godly wisdom must be like our love—demonstrated in word and truth. In other words, our lives must back up our testimonies. And this only follows the consistent message of the book of James, that "faith without works is dead" (2:20).

Sixth, heavenly wisdom is without partiality. The term used here describes someone who is not discriminatory toward others.

Seventh, heavenly wisdom is without hypocrisy. The word *hypocrisy* comes from the world of drama. In the first-century world, when a person played a part on stage and wore mask, he or she was called a hypocrite. The term gradually became associated with folks who played a role off stage as well. Today, a hypocrite is someone who is not real—who is phony and does not truly represent himself or herself.

So, what do we represent? Worldly wisdom or earthly wisdom? If we are going to walk with Christ, we have to be different than those who walk by the wisdom of the world. But God wouldn't set this before us without the potential for us to do it in His power. We can live in His wisdom if we fill our hearts with His truth, for little by little, His truth will take over our lives and we will be people walking after the wisdom of God.

JOURNALING YOUR RESPONSE

What are some areas of your life right now where you could use more of God's wisdom?

THE ROOT OF CONFLICTS

James 4:1–10

GETTING STARTED

What are some causes of tension among people that you have witnessed in your life?

_____

_____

_____

_____

_____

_____

_____

_____

_____

_____

_____

_____

_____

_____

_____

_____

_____

_____

_____

_____

_____

SETTING THE STAGE

History reveals that conflicts among God's people have existed for as long as God's people have assembled together. In the book of Acts, we read that one of the earliest disputes was between two groups of Jewish Christians, whom Luke calls the *Hebrews* and the *Hellenists*. As he writes, "Now in those days, when the number of the disciples was multiplying, there arose a complaint against the Hebrews by the Hellenists, because their widows were neglected in the daily distribution" (6:1).

Later, disputes in the church broke out between the Jewish Christians and those from non-Jewish backgrounds, whom Luke calls the *Gentiles*. This resulted in a special council being convened in Jerusalem to resolve the matter (see Acts 15:6–29). The apostle Paul also had to frequently step in to resolve disputes among his Gentile churches (see, for example 1 Corinthians 1:10–17).

In this next section of James, we see that he also felt the need to address divisions in the church that were causing dissention and strife. James even seeks to identify the root of those conflicts. Recall that James has just documented the results of God's wisdom at work in the life of a believer: an outflowing of peace, righteousness, and other godly virtues (see James 3:17–18). But the wisdom of the world also has byproducts! When this worldly wisdom is set free in the church, it will bring about evil results—including conflict among believers.

James wastes little time in getting to the heart of the matter: "Where do wars and fights come from among you? Do they not come from your desires for pleasure that war in your members?" (4:1). In the Greek, the word that James uses for *pleasures* is *hedone*—from which we derive *hedonism*. Hedonism is simply the pleasure derived from fulfilling one's own desires. James saw hedonism as a negative force that led to *pride*—putting one's own needs above the needs of the group—and recognized it as the source of many conflicts in the church.

Hedonism still exists in the church today . . . as do conflicts among believers. Perhaps this is why James's words in this section of his letter resonate with us so powerfully. They reveal our struggles with pride and self-interest and compel us to seek God's way instead.

EXPLORING THE TEXT

Pride Promotes Strife (James 4:1–5)

> [1] Where do wars and fights come from among you? Do they not come from your desires for pleasure that war in your members? [2] You lust and do not have. You murder and covet and cannot obtain. You fight and war. Yet you do not have because you do not ask. [3] You ask and do not receive, because you ask amiss, that you may spend it on your pleasures. [4] Adulterers and adulteresses! Do you not know that friendship with the world is enmity with God? Whoever therefore wants to be a friend of the world makes himself an enemy of God. [5] Or do you think that the Scripture says in vain, "The Spirit who dwells in us yearns jealously"?

1. James identifies the source of conflicts in the church as arising from the members' desire to put their needs above the needs of the community. What does he say are the consequences? Why weren't they seeing their prayers answered (see verses 1–3)?

_____

_____

_____

_____

_____

_____

_____

2. James identifies his readers as "adulterers and adulteresses," which emphasizes that they had given themselves over to other "gods"—in this case, their own lusts and desires. What does the resulting friendship with the world bring (see verses 4–5)?

_____

_____

_____

_____

_____

_____

_____

_____

_____

Humility Cures Worldliness (James 4:6–10)

⁶ But He gives more grace. Therefore He says:

"God resists the proud,
But gives grace to the humble."

⁷ Therefore submit to God. Resist the devil and he will flee from you. ⁸ Draw near to God and He will draw near to you. Cleanse your hands, you sinners; and purify your hearts, you double-minded. ⁹ Lament and mourn and weep! Let your laughter be turned to mourning and your joy to gloom. ¹⁰ Humble yourselves in the sight of the Lord, and He will lift you up.

3. James has been forthright in identifying the problem. Now he will be just as forthright in identifying the solution. What are the first steps that must be taken by members in the congregation to start to heal the divisions in the church (see verses 6–7)?

_____

_____

_____

_____

_____

_____

_____

4. The word *double-minded* in verse 8 refers to people whose divided commitment and questionable loyalties cause them to be spiritually unstable. What attitude changes are necessary in order to become "single-minded" (see verses 8–10)?

_____

_____

_____

_____

_____

_____

_____

_____

GOING DEEPER

The cure that James proposes for divisions in the church is *humility*. As someone once said, "Humility isn't thinking less of yourself—it's thinking of yourself less." When we think of ourselves *less*, it naturally leads to us thinking of others *more*. We begin to consider their needs and how our actions will impact them. Other authors of the New Testament saw this same correlation, as indicated in the following passages from the apostle Paul and from John.

Graces of the Heirs of Grace (Titus 3:1–7)

¹ Remind them to be subject to rulers and authorities, to obey, to be ready for every good work, ² to speak evil of no one, to be peaceable, gentle, showing all humility to all men. ³ For we ourselves were also once foolish, disobedient, deceived, serving various lusts and pleasures, living in malice and envy, hateful and hating one another. ⁴ But when the kindness and the love of God our Savior toward man appeared, ⁵ not by works of righteousness which we have done, but according to His mercy He saved us, through the washing of regeneration and renewing of the Holy Spirit, ⁶ whom He poured out on us abundantly through Jesus Christ our Savior, ⁷ that having been justified by His grace we should become heirs according to the hope of eternal life.

5. Paul states that believers should be "peaceable, gentle, showing humility to all men" (verse 2). How does he describe our condition before we came to Christ? How would these traits lead to conflicts if they were not put to death in our lives (see verses 1–3)?

6. Paul reminds us that salvation comes only from the love and kindness of God—there is nothing we can do to earn it (see verses 4–7). How should this realization lead to humility?

_____

_____

_____

_____

_____

_____

Do Not Love the World (1 John 2:15–17)

¹⁵ Do not love the world or the things in the world. If anyone loves the world, the love of the Father is not in him. ¹⁶ For all that is in the world—the lust of the flesh, the lust of the eyes, and the pride of life—is not of the Father but is of the world. ¹⁷ And the world is passing away, and the lust of it; but he who does the will of God abides forever.

7. When John advises that we should not love the world, he is referring to the morally evil system that opposes the things of God. What is the inescapable result of loving the things of the world (see verses 15–16)?

_____

_____

_____

_____

_____

_____

8. "The lust of the flesh" refers to the desire for sensual pleasure, "the lust of the eyes" to covetousness, and "the pride of life" to being impressed with one's position in the world. Why is it important to resist the allure of these temporary pleasures (see verses 16–17)?

_____

_____

_____

_____

_____

REVIEWING THE STORY

James traces the origin of the conflict in the church to the selfish desire for pleasure. Such desires can cause us to become double-minded and interfere with our prayers. What is more, our friendliness with the things of this world makes us enemies of God. Humility is the cure to this problem and the key to restoring our relationship with God. When we humbly submit to God and resist the temptations of the devil, the Lord draws closer to us. He bestows His grace on us and equips us to honor Him in our interpersonal relationships.

9. What is the cause of the wars and fights that ruin our relationships (see James 4:1)?

_____

_____

_____

_____

_____

10. What happens when we make requests to God from selfish motives (see James 4:3)?

11. What is the promise when we submit to God and draw near to Him (see James 4:7–8)?

12. What happens when we choose to humble ourselves before God (see James 4:10)?

APPLYING THE MESSAGE

13. What are some of the ways that God has taught you humility in your life?

_____

_____

_____

_____

_____

_____

_____

_____

14. How can you ensure that you are not making requests of God based on selfish motives?

_____

_____

_____

_____

_____

_____

_____

REFLECTING ON THE MEANING

James provides an interesting remedy in this section for the conflicts that were erupting in the early church. While we might assume he would advise his readers to work out the problem among themselves, or take it to the pastor, or seek help from an arbitrator, he instead reminds them that they have been given a gift from God called *grace*. They did nothing to earn it . . . nor could they do anything to earn it.

This realization should have caused them to think less highly of themselves and more of others. But instead, we find that personal pride had crept into the communities. The believers needed to get rid of this spirit of pride and entitlement, which God opposes, and get back to the basics of loving and serving one another. So, James provides them with four practical steps they can make to implement this shift in their hearts and lives.

First, relinquish control to God. James simply states, "Therefore submit to God" (4:7). The word *submit* means to "take rank under" or "yield to a superior force." James understood the believers would not be having these conflicts if they were truly submitting to God. For if they were, they would be putting God first and looking out for the needs of others.

Second, reject sinful attitudes. James instructs, "purify your hearts, you double-minded" (verse 8). The term that James invokes here expresses fickleness and vacillation. It describes the person who wants to love God but also keeps a foot in the world. It is this type of attitude that will keep the grace of God from flowing in the life of the Christian.

Third, refrain from frivolous attitudes. James writes, "Let your laughter be turned to mourning and your joy to gloom" (verse 9). Now, James is not suggesting that Christians should dress in black clothing and walk around with a somber face. Christians should be happy in the Lord and thankful for the gift of salvation. But when they have fallen into sin, they need to recognize the seriousness of their condition. Laughter and joy are silenced for a season.

Fourth, refuse to slander others. "Do not speak evil of one another" (verse 11). The chief work of Satan is to slander God's people. So, when we speak evil of other believers, we are doing the devil's work. Conflicts come from our own self-centeredness. For this reason, we need to ask God to put a guard before our lips so that we don't say hurtful things about others.

As we take these steps, we will begin to adopt an attitude of humility. We will resist the pull of pride in our lives. We will naturally love others. And we will honor God in the process.

JOURNALING YOUR RESPONSE

How will you start to implement each of these steps into your life this week?

PLANNING YOUR FUTURE

James 4:11–17

GETTING STARTED

What concerns you the most about the future?

_____

_____

_____

_____

_____

_____

_____

_____

_____

_____

_____

_____

_____

_____

SETTING THE STAGE

Some of us would give anything to know what the future holds for us. We want know where we will live, what job we will hold, and generally where we will be in life ten . . . fifteen . . . and even twenty years down the road.

While that may seem like a harmless diversion, often there is something deeper at work when we long for some foreknowledge of what lies ahead. Many times, what we want from God is just enough for us *not* to have to rely on Him all the time.

However, from the beginning, God has shown that His preferred method is daily dependence on Him. For example, when the Israelites left Egypt during the exodus, the Lord did not give them transports full of food and drink for their journey across the wilderness. He preferred to give, in His own faithful way, enough for one day at a time. Likewise, God does not fully reveal our future to us but gives us just what we need to face each day as it comes.

God does this for our own good. Augustine, one of the early church fathers, put it this way: "God will not suffer man to have the knowledge of things to come, for if he had awareness of his prosperity, he would be careless; and understanding his adversity, he would be senseless." God does not want us to be complacent or to get caught up in worry. Instead, He wants us to stay focused on Him—and trust in Him—in both the good times and the bad.

In this next section of James, the author reminds us that while we cannot predict the future, we can learn how to face it. We should never plan our lives without taking God into consideration, nor should we presume a certain future when we have no control over it. We must not convince ourselves that we are sufficient to face life armed only with our own wisdom and strength. The mistakes that James's original readers were making are often repeated by modern Christians. So, the instructions James gave them will surely be helpful to us today.

EXPLORING THE TEXT

Do Not Judge a Brother (James 4:11–12)

¹¹ Do not speak evil of one another, brethren. He who speaks evil of a brother and judges his brother, speaks evil of the law and judges

the law. But if you judge the law, you are not a doer of the law but a judge. [12] There is one Lawgiver, who is able to save and to destroy. Who are you to judge another?

---

1. James has just advised his readers to submit to God and live in humility. Part of being humble requires them to not judge others—to not see themselves as better than their brothers and sisters in Christ. The Old Testament law forbids spreading slander: "You shall not go about as a talebearer among your people" (Leviticus 19:16). What does James say the believers are actually doing when they slander one another (see James 4:11)?

_____

_____

_____

_____

_____

2. James notes that "there is one Lawgiver." God *alone* has the power to bring salvation or judgment. With that in mind, what question should guide our actions when we are tempted to disregard His law and speak evil of other people (see verse 12)?

_____

_____

_____

_____

_____

_____

_____

Do Not Boast About Tomorrow (James 4:13–17)

¹³ Come now, you who say, "Today or tomorrow we will go to such and such a city, spend a year there, buy and sell, and make a profit"; ¹⁴ whereas you do not know what will happen tomorrow. For what is your life? It is even a vapor that appears for a little time and then vanishes away. ¹⁵ Instead you ought to say, "If the Lord wills, we shall live and do this or that." ¹⁶ But now you boast in your arrogance. All such boasting is evil.

¹⁷ Therefore, to him who knows to do good and does not do it, to him it is sin.

3. Another part of being humble involves not "boasting" about the future. Here James is addressing the movers and shakers of the first-century business world. These people could afford to move their operations from one city to another to take advantage of market trends. What was the flaw in their planning for the future (see verses 13–14)?

4. In the Bible, we find that God will either reveal His will in certain instances or keep it hidden. His revealed will involves His mandates for righteous living that are found in Scripture. James's reference here is to God's hidden will, which is like a veil covering the future. What is the best way to account for God's hidden will (see verses 15–17)?

_____

_____

_____

_____

_____

_____

_____

_____

_____

GOING DEEPER

James was not discouraging his readers from making plans for the future. In fact, in the Bible we read that "the plans of the diligent lead surely to plenty" (Proverbs 21:5). But James was encouraging his readers not to be presumptuous in their planning and to submit those plans to the Lord. Solomon, the wisest man who ever lived, comments on this in the following passage.

The Fear of the Lord Leads to Life (Proverbs 19:20–23)

[20] Listen to counsel and receive instruction,
That you may be wise in your latter days.

[21] There are many plans in a man's heart,
Nevertheless the LORD's counsel—that will stand.

²² What is desired in a man is kindness,
And a poor man is better than a liar.

²³ The fear of the LORD leads to life,
And he who has it will abide in satisfaction;
He will not be visited with evil.

---

5. What steps does Solomon advise we take when making plans? What determines whether our plans for the future will stand or fall (see verses 20–21)?

_____

_____

_____

_____

_____

_____

6. The word *fear* refers to holding the Lord in great awe and respect. What happens to those who choose to live their lives in fear of the Lord (see verses 22–23)?

_____

_____

_____

_____

_____

_____

Jesus also addresses this concept of including God in our plans and not presuming that a certain future will happen. In the following passage, he discusses this from the perspective of *worry*. At its core, worry is assuming the worst will happen. It compels us to fear what lies ahead and represents a lack of trust that God can bring good into it. Jesus points out the futility of trying to micromanage the future through worry and encourages us to instead have faith in God.

Do Not Worry (Matthew 6:25–34)

[25] "Therefore I say to you, do not worry about your life, what you will eat or what you will drink; nor about your body, what you will put on. Is not life more than food and the body more than clothing? [26] Look at the birds of the air, for they neither sow nor reap nor gather into barns; yet your heavenly Father feeds them. Are you not of more value than they? [27] Which of you by worrying can add one cubit to his stature?

[28] "So why do you worry about clothing? Consider the lilies of the field, how they grow: they neither toil nor spin; [29] and yet I say to you that even Solomon in all his glory was not arrayed like one of these. [30] Now if God so clothes the grass of the field, which today is, and tomorrow is thrown into the oven, will He not much more clothe you, O you of little faith?

[31] "Therefore do not worry, saying, 'What shall we eat?' or 'What shall we drink?' or 'What shall we wear?' [32] For after all these things the Gentiles seek. For your heavenly Father knows that you need all these things. [33] But seek first the kingdom of God and His righteousness, and all these things shall be added to you. [34] Therefore do not worry about tomorrow, for tomorrow will worry about its own things. Sufficient for the day is its own trouble."

7. Jesus reminds us in this passage that God is our heavenly *Father,* and like all good fathers, He knows that we have basic needs in life that have to be met. What do His examples of the "birds of the air" and the "lilies of the field" reveal about how God cares for us? What is Jesus' point in calling out these illustrations as it relates to worry (see verses 25–30)?

_____

_____

_____

_____

_____

_____

_____

_____

8. *Gentiles,* in this context, refers to people who did not know God. The Jewish people, because of God's revelation to them, were supposed to think differently than the Gentiles. What should be the attitude of God's people when it comes to their future? What should be their primary focus in life (see verses 31–34)?

_____

_____

_____

_____

_____

_____

_____

REVIEWING THE STORY

James touches on two problems involving the wealthier members of the church: slander and boasting. The members knew that slander was forbidden by Old Testament law. By disregarding the command, they were, in essence, acting as judges over the law. As for boasting, they were placing too much confidence in their own plans. James points out that only God knows the future—and can change it at any time. So, these members needed to stop boasting about what the future held and instead live according to God's will on a day-to-day basis.

9. What happens when we speak evil of our Christian brothers and sisters (see James 4:11)?

_____

_____

_____

_____

_____

_____

_____

10. What was the attitude of some of the wealthier members of the church (see James 4:13)?

_____

_____

_____

_____

_____

_____

_____

_____

_____

11. What image does James use to illustrate the fragile nature of human life (see James 4:14)?

_____

_____

_____

_____

_____

12. How can believers show a humble attitude when it comes to the future (see James 4:15)?

_____

_____

_____

_____

_____

_____

APPLYING THE MESSAGE

13. What strategies help you to not judge others or engage in gossip about them?

_____

_____

_____

_____

_____

_____

14. What plans do you have for the next year? How have you involved God in those plans?

_____

_____

_____

_____

REFLECTING ON THE MEANING

James opened his letter by calling out the rich and instructing them to pursue humility: "Let the lowly brother glory in his exaltation, but the rich in his humiliation" (1:9–10). In this section, he now addresses their arrogance in believing they were the masters of their own fate: "You do not know what will happen tomorrow . . . you boast in your arrogance" (4:14, 16).

In the original Greek, the word that James uses for *boast* is plural. This indicates that he is referring to *many* outbursts of pride and bragging from these wealthier members. They we running their lives apart from God . . . and they were proud of it. James is clear on how God considered their attitude: "All such boasting is evil" (verse 16).

If we are honest, we have to admit that we all have fallen into this pattern at times. Fortunately, James does not just give us these warnings but also provides us with an alternative to explore. As he writes, "Instead, you ought to say, 'If the Lord wills, we shall live and do this or that'" (verse 15). The appropriate response to the uncertain nature of the future is to humbly submit our will to God's and to completely rely on Him.

If you had the opportunity to read letters that passed between Christians a few hundred years ago, you would notice the postscript "D. V." These two letters stand for the Latin words *Deo Volente*, which mean "if the Lord wills" or "God willing." It was a reminder to both the writer and the recipient that God is ultimately in control of any plans they made. This should be our mindset regarding the future as well—always with the words "God willing" on our minds.

JOURNALING YOUR RESPONSE

What are some of the ways that you have seen God direct your plans?

JUSTICE AND ENDURANCE

James 5:1–11

GETTING STARTED

What are some things that most try your patience?

_____

_____

_____

_____

_____

_____

_____

_____

_____

_____

_____

_____

SETTING THE STAGE

The Lotte New York Palace Hotel is a luxury establishment located in midtown Manhattan. Prior to 1992, it was known as The Helmsley Palace Hotel—a name that brings to mind one of the more bizarre tales of the 1980s. Built in 1974, the hotel was managed by Leona Helmsley. Nicknamed the "Queen of Mean," she maintained a strict management style that involved firing staff members for trivial mistakes and basically treating them like dirt. She also did not like to pay her taxes—a fact that led to her conviction for tax evasion in a federal court.

One would think that with all the money Leona possessed, the least she could have done was treat her people with decency. But the sad truth is that there is something about the love of money for its own sake that brings out the worst in people. Numerous examples of this are given in Scripture, including Achan (see Joshua 7), Delilah (see Judges 16), Solomon (see Deuteronomy 17:16–17), and in the ultimate act of treachery, Judas (see Matthew 26:14–16).

However, this passage is not an indictment on wealth. There is no data in the Bible that supports the idea that it is wrong to be wealthy. In fact, there is evidence to the contrary. In Proverbs we read, "The blessing of the Lord makes one rich, and He adds no sorrow with it" (Proverbs 10:22). Numerous examples are provided in Scripture of people who were both wealthy and godly, including Job, Abraham, Nicodemus, and Joseph of Arimathea.

God does not disapprove of people with money, but He does speak out against those who trust in their own riches instead of Him. This uncontrolled desire for wealth is the target of James' sweeping statements in this chapter. Like Paul, the danger he sees is not in wealth itself but in loving wealth so much that it blocks out love for God and for others (see 1 Timothy 6:10). Let's see what James has to say about people who do not honor God with their wealth.

EXPLORING THE TEXT

Rich Oppressors Will Be Judged (James 5:1–6)

¹ Come now, you rich, weep and howl for your miseries that are coming upon you! ²Your riches are corrupted, and your garments are

moth-eaten. ³ Your gold and silver are corroded, and their corrosion will be a witness against you and will eat your flesh like fire. You have heaped up treasure in the last days. ⁴ Indeed the wages of the laborers who mowed your fields, which you kept back by fraud, cry out; and the cries of the reapers have reached the ears of the Lord of Sabaoth. ⁵ You have lived on the earth in pleasure and luxury; you have fattened your hearts as in a day of slaughter. ⁶ You have condemned, you have murdered the just; he does not resist you.

---

1. One of the issues that James had with the wealthy merchants in the church was in regard to the way they treated others—especially the laborers who worked for them. These merchants were notorious for using their money to buy off courts and pervert justice. But how will the court of God's judgment turn their wealth against them (see verses 2–3)?

_____

_____

_____

_____

_____

_____

2. The term *laborers* refers to the poorer members of the church. How did the wealthy merchants' treatment of these laborers testify against them (see verses 4–6)?

_____

_____

_____

_____

_____

_____

_____

Be Patient and Persevering (James 5:7–11)

⁷ Therefore be patient, brethren, until the coming of the Lord. See how the farmer waits for the precious fruit of the earth, waiting patiently for it until it receives the early and latter rain. ⁸ You also be patient. Establish your hearts, for the coming of the Lord is at hand.

⁹ Do not grumble against one another, brethren, lest you be condemned. Behold, the Judge is standing at the door! ¹⁰ My brethren, take the prophets, who spoke in the name of the Lord, as an example of suffering and patience. ¹¹ Indeed we count them blessed who endure. You have heard of the perseverance of Job and seen the end intended by the Lord—that the Lord is very compassionate and merciful.

3. The statements James makes about these wealthy members of the church would have encouraged the less-wealthy laborers that God was aware of their plight. James will now take this message one step further by encouraging these members to continue to endure. What is his advice to these people who are hoping for justice (see verses 7–8)?

_____

_____

_____

_____

_____

_____

_____

_____

_____

_____

_____

_____

4. The word that James uses for *grumble* in verse 9 can also be translated as "sigh or groan." He tells these members of the church to persevere and not give in to despair, for God, the great Judge, is standing just on the other side of the door. What does James say will happen to those who continue to endure and persevere for Christ (see verses 9–11)?

_____

_____

_____

_____

_____

_____

_____

_____

Going Deeper

As previously noted, James is not offering general indictment on wealth in this passage. Rather, his warning is about people's *attitude* toward their riches. His words in many ways echo the teaching from Jesus on laying up treasures in heaven that He gave in the Sermon on the Mount.

The Proper Pursuit (Matthew 6:19–24)

¹⁹ "Do not lay up for yourselves treasures on earth, where moth and rust destroy and where thieves break in and steal; ²⁰ but lay up for yourselves treasures in heaven, where neither moth nor rust destroys and where thieves do not break in and steal. ²¹ For where your treasure is, there your heart will be also.

²² "The lamp of the body is the eye. If therefore your eye is good, your whole body will be full of light. ²³ But if your eye is bad, your

whole body will be full of darkness. If therefore the light that is in you is darkness, how great is that darkness!

[24] "No one can serve two masters; for either he will hate the one and love the other, or else he will be loyal to the one and despise the other. You cannot serve God and mammon."

---

5. Jesus states that His followers are not to give priority to the pursuit of earthly treasures. What should our attitude be instead (see verses 19–21)?

_____

_____

_____

_____

_____

_____

_____

_____

_____

6. The term *mammon* simply means wealth, money, or property. What happens when God and mammon make opposing demands us (see verses 22–24)?

_____

_____

_____

_____

_____

_____

_____

_____

Other leaders in the early church also saw the danger in placing one's trust in earthly possessions. In Paul's first letter to Timothy, he issues a passionate plea for believers in Christ to be content with what God has provided to them and to avoid seeking after worldly riches. Paul peeled back the shiny veneer of this pursuit of wealth to reveal its ugly underbelly.

Error and Greed (1 Timothy 6:6–10)

> [6] Now godliness with contentment is great gain. [7] For we brought nothing into this world, and it is certain we can carry nothing out. [8] And having food and clothing, with these we shall be content. [9] But those who desire to be rich fall into temptation and a snare, and into many foolish and harmful lusts which drown men in destruction and perdition. [10] For the love of money is a root of all kinds of evil, for which some have strayed from the faith in their greediness, and pierced themselves through with many sorrows.

7. Paul states that the sign of godliness in a person's life is contentment with their state in life. What is necessary to achieve contentment (see verses 6–8)?

_____

_____

_____

_____

_____

_____

_____

_____

_____

8. Paul uses the phrase *many sorrows* at the end of this passage to emphasize the reality that a life focused solely on seeking material gain only produces pain. What is the greatest danger for believers who are enticed by earthly riches (see verses 9–10)?

_____

_____

_____

_____

_____

Reviewing the Story

James continues to pronounce judgment on the wealthy members of the church who had gained their riches by exploiting and taking advantage of laborers. He envisions a courtroom setting in which the material possessions these wealthy merchants have pursued at all costs now testify against them. James then urges patience for those who long for God's judgment against such actions. He uses examples from nature and the endurance of Old Testament prophets to remind us that God rewards patience and perseverance in the midst of suffering.

9. What warnings does James issue to the wealthy people in the church (see James 5:1–3)?

_____

_____

_____

_____

_____

_____

10. For what offenses will the wealthy people be judged
(see James 5:4–6)?

_____

_____

_____

_____

_____

_____

11. What analogy does James use to illustrate how God rewards
patience (see James 5:7–8)?

_____

_____

_____

_____

_____

_____

12. What spiritual truth should give us hope as we endure patiently
(see James 5:11)?

_____

_____

_____

_____

_____

_____

APPLYING THE MESSAGE

13. What is your attitude when it comes to earthly wealth and possessions?

_____

_____

_____

_____

_____

_____

_____

_____

14. How has God helped you to endure even during times of suffering?

_____

_____

_____

_____

_____

_____

_____

_____

REFLECTING ON THE MEANING

Patience is in short supply in today's fast-paced world. We consider our time to be precious, so we get aggravated when we have to wait in lines at the bank, or at the supermarket, or in traffic on the freeway. But James proposes a different course. In this section of his letter, he highlights the value of instead exhibiting *patience* in three key areas of life.

First, when we face difficulty. James writes, "Therefore be patient, brethren, until the coming of the Lord. See how the farmer waits for the precious fruit of the earth, waiting patiently for it until it receives the early and latter rain. You also be patient" (5:7–8). The wicked wealthy had committed many injustices against the believers. But James reminds them that no matter what evil has been done to them, they are not to retaliate. The word James uses for *patience* literally means to be long-suffering. As farmers wait for rain, so believers must live in anticipation of the Lord's return and not get upset when times are difficult.

Second, when we face disappointment. James states, "Do not grumble against one another, brethren, lest you be condemned" (verse 9). James is speaking here about how we are to act toward other believers when facing difficulty. When we begin to feel the heat, our first reaction is typically to complain and lash out against others. Instead, James says we are to exhibit *restraint*. Just as farmers help one another in good times and bad, so believers in Christ are to stick together in all situations. When pressures mount, there is a temptation to divide, but it is at such times that the family of God must come together.

Third, when we face disapproval. James notes, "My brethren, take the prophets, who spoke in the name of the Lord, as an example of suffering and patience. Indeed we count them blessed who endure" (verses 10–11). James's point is that the prophets did not suffer because they did anything *wrong* but because they were doing *right*. They were disapproved of by their contemporaries and persecuted for their testimony. James likewise knew what it meant to suffer. These prophets to whom he refers were—like him—suffering affliction with patience.

Life will not get easier for any of us. It only gets harder. But in the difficulties of life, we need to learn these lessons of patience. We need to trust that the One who has called us is faithful and will sustain us through the difficult steps as we patiently endure for Him.

JOURNALING YOUR RESPONSE

When have you experienced this kind "second wind" in your life?

LESSON *twelve*

REASONS TO PRAY
James 5:12–20

GETTING STARTED

At what times and in what situations are you most likely to pray?

_____
_____
_____
_____
_____
_____
_____
_____
_____
_____
_____
_____

SETTING THE STAGE

If ever a man was qualified to address the subject of prayer, it was James. He is portrayed by an ancient writer as a man whose times of prayer for his nation were frequent and prolonged. As the tradition states, James used to enter the temple alone, without any fanfare, and could be found kneeling and praying for forgiveness of his people. It is said that because of his constant kneeling during his long sessions of prayer, he even developed knots on his knees. Over time, his knees grew calloused, and people referred to him as "Old Camel Knees." The nickname was his reward for his constant prayerful concern for God's people!

Most of us find it hard to identify with a man like James. After all, what people do we know in our lives who pray so much that they develop knots on their knees? Perhaps the better question is simply whom do we know in our lives who *actually* pray at all. This is not an unfair question . . . nor is it calculated to trigger guilt. It simply reflects the reality that people today tend to believe that they are just too busy to pray.

As James closes his letter, we find one of the strongest passages on prayer in the New Testament. In the author's previous discussion on perseverance, he used the word *patient* or *patience* four times in just five verses (see 5:7–12). In this passage, he uses the word *pray* or *prayer* seven times (see verses 13–18). The placement of these two passages is far from accidental, for there is a strong connection between patience and prayer.

Often, the situations in life that call for patience are the ones that trigger emotions within us like anger, fear, or doubt. Our first instinct will be to react based on these emotions—to lash out, or worry, or try to avoid the situation entirely. But a wiser course is respond by going to the One who can see the big picture. Thus, James's point in the final section of his letter is that when situations arise in which patience is required . . . *prayer* is the key.

EXPLORING THE TEXT

Meeting Specific Needs (James 5:12–15)

12 But above all, my brethren, do not swear, either by heaven or by earth or with any other oath. But let your "Yes" be "Yes," and your "No," "No," lest you fall into judgment.

¹³ Is anyone among you suffering? Let him pray. Is anyone cheerful? Let him sing psalms. ¹⁴ Is anyone among you sick? Let him call for the elders of the church, and let them pray over him, anointing him with oil in the name of the Lord. ¹⁵ And the prayer of faith will save the sick, and the Lord will raise him up. And if he has committed sins, he will be forgiven.

1. James echoes Jesus' words in the Sermon on the Mount: "You shall not swear falsely . . . but let your 'Yes' be 'Yes,' and your 'No,' 'No'" (Matthew 5:33, 37). At that time, much like today, people would make oaths to "prove" that what they were saying was trustworthy and true. What do James and Jesus advise believers to do instead (see verse 12)?

2. James has focused throughout his letter on the believer's response to suffering and trials in life. In this passage, he comes to the conclusion that the ultimate response should be going to God in prayer. In what situations are we to pray? What is the promise for those who take such a cheerful response to adversity (see verses 13–15)?

Bring Back the Erring One (James 5:16–20)

¹⁶ Confess your trespasses to one another, and pray for one another, that you may be healed. The effective, fervent prayer of a righteous man avails much. ¹⁷ Elijah was a man with a nature like ours, and he prayed earnestly that it would not rain; and it did not rain on the land for three years and six months. ¹⁸ And he prayed again, and the heaven gave rain, and the earth produced its fruit.

¹⁹ Brethren, if anyone among you wanders from the truth, and someone turns him back, ²⁰ let him know that he who turns a sinner from the error of his way will save a soul from death and cover a multitude of sins.

3. James ends his letter with an exhortation for believers to put his words into practice. What remedies does he suggest for healing fractured relationships? How does the example of Elijah demonstrate the power of a fervent prayer (see verses 16–18)?

_____

_____

_____

_____

_____

_____

_____

_____

4. The final instruction that James gives is on lovingly rebuking the church member who has fallen into a pattern of sin. The phrase *cover a multitude of sins* alludes to Proverbs 10:12 and likely refers to suppression or prevention of future sins the person might commit.

What is the blessing given on the one who helps another believer in this way (see verses 19–20)?

_____

_____

_____

_____

_____

_____

_____

Going Deeper

The topic of prayer was important not only to James but also to other authors of the New Testament. Paul, in particular, was always careful to point out the need for prayer in the church and to extol believers in Christ to continually be seeking God as they went about their day. Like James, the apostle Paul often closed out his epistles with specific admonitions for believers in Christ to never neglect prayer, as the following passages relate.

Prayer and Sanctification (1 Thessalonians 5:16–25)

16 Rejoice always, 17 pray without ceasing, 18 in everything give thanks; for this is the will of God in Christ Jesus for you.

19 Do not quench the Spirit. 20 Do not despise prophecies. 21 Test all things; hold fast what is good. 22 Abstain from every form of evil.

23 Now may the God of peace Himself sanctify you completely; and may your whole spirit, soul, and body be preserved blameless at the coming of our Lord Jesus Christ. 24 He who calls you is faithful, who also will do it.

25 Brethren, pray for us.

5. Joy is possible not because of the circumstances we face but because we trust in a God who is sovereign and working out His good purposes in every situation. What should be our attitude when we pray? What does it mean to "not quench the Spirit" (see verses 16–19)?

_____

_____

_____

_____

6. What other instructions does the apostle Paul provide to believers in this passage? What is his own prayer for the believers in this city (see verses 20–20)?

_____

_____

_____

_____

_____

Anxious for Nothing (Philippians 4:6–9)

⁶ Be anxious for nothing, but in everything by prayer and supplication, with thanksgiving, let your requests be made known to God; ⁷ and the peace of God, which surpasses all understanding, will guard your hearts and minds through Christ Jesus.

⁸ Finally, brethren, whatever things are true, whatever things are noble, whatever things are just, whatever things are pure, whatever things are lovely, whatever things are of good report, if there is any virtue and if there is anything praiseworthy—meditate on these things. ⁹ The things which you learned and received and heard and saw in me, these do, and the God of peace will be with you.

7. Paul draws on Jesus' instruction to "not worry about your life" (Matthew 6:25) and to instead look to God to provide for all our needs. What does Paul say will occur when we present our requests to God and trust that He will deliver (see Philippians 4:6–7)?

_____

_____

_____

_____

_____

_____

8. Paul instructs us to turn to God in prayer when we are in need or are worried about the future—and to trust that God will provide for us. What additional step does Paul say that we need to take as it relates to our attitude and thoughts (see verses 8–9)?

_____

_____

_____

_____

_____

_____

REVIEWING THE STORY

James closes his letter by challenging his readers to reverse their negative patterns of speech. He advises them to not take oaths to "prove" they are trustworthy but to practice plain speaking, to pray, and to sing psalms. He encourages believers to get involved in one another's lives. This includes the elders of the church taking care of the sick, the church members confessing their sins to one another, and the congregation seeking the Lord for forgiveness. James closes by reminding his readers about the extraordinary impact of the prophet Elijah's prayers and the opportunity they all have to turn sinners from their destructive ways.

9. What kind of plain speaking does James encourage believers to pursue (see James 5:12)?

_____

_____

_____

_____

_____

10. What do suffering, sickness, and cheerfulness have in common (see James 5:13–15)?

_____

_____

_____

_____

_____

11. What does James say about the prayer of a righteous person (see James 5:16)?

_____

_____

_____

_____

_____

12. What should believers do when they see others turn away from the faith (see James 5:19–20)?

_____

_____

_____

_____

_____

_____

APPLYING THE MESSAGE

13. How do the people in your life know that you are trustworthy in all you say and do?

_____

_____

_____

_____

_____

_____

_____

14. When are times that God has miraculously provided for you when you prayed?

_____

_____

_____

_____

_____

_____

_____

REFLECTING ON THE MEANING

In this final section of James, the author concludes his letter by imploring his readers to take all of their needs and requests to God in prayer. He identifies at least three reasons why every believer needs to make prayer a cornerstone of every aspect of life.

First, there is an emotional reason. James asks, "Is anyone among you suffering?" (verse 13). He is referring here to hardships and distresses that involve mental or emotional suffering. Prayer is the best response to such stressors in our lives. James also asks in this same verse, "Is anyone cheerful?" Cheerfulness also calls for prayer—in the form of "psalms" or songs of worship to God. Praising the Lord in song is a valid and necessary manner of praying.

Second, there is a physical reason. James asks, "Is anyone among you sick?" (verse 14). Here he is talking about serious physical illness. His remedy is prayer—specifically, the prayers of the church elders. The image James presents is one of church leaders who are ready to prayerfully respond when they are summoned. They pray over the sick and anoint them with oil that has medicinal value. So, God's healing comes through the prayers of others and through medicinal means. The church leaders were not divine healers but instruments of prayer.

Third, there is a spiritual reason. James urges prayerful confession as an instrument of healing (see verses 15–16). God sometimes uses physical maladies to discipline us for sin, and confession allows us to isolate the offense. When the sin is isolated and confessed, it can be forgiven. Another spiritual reason for prayer in the body of Christ is the common experience of believers who fall into patterns of sin. James puts the responsibility for the wandering brother or sister on the shoulders of the church. Our prayers can work wonders in the lives of others!

James's final message to us is this: *God still answers prayer.* Whether our prayers are in the emotional, physical, or spiritual realm, God is ready to hear and willing to answer. As James states, "The effective, fervent prayer of a righteous man avails much" (verse 16).

JOURNALING YOUR RESPONSE

How would you summarize the need for prayer in the life of a Christian?

LEADER'S GUIDE

Thank you for choosing to lead your group through this study from Dr. David Jeremiah on *The Letter of James*. Being a group leader has its own rewards, and it is our prayer that your walk with the Lord will deepen through this experience. During the twelve lessons in this study, you and your group will read selected passages from James, explore key themes in the letter based on teachings from Dr. Jeremiah, and review questions that will encourage group discussion. There are multiple components in this section that can help you structure your lessons and discussion time, so please be sure to read and consider each one.

BEFORE YOU BEGIN

Before your first meeting, make sure you and your group are well-versed with the content of the lesson. Group members should have their own copy of *The Letter of James* study guide prior to the first meeting so they can follow along and record their answers, thoughts, and insights. After the first week, you may wish to assign the study guide lesson as homework prior to the group meeting and then use the meeting time to discuss the content in the lesson.

To ensure everyone has a chance to participate in the discussion, the ideal size for a group is around eight to ten people. If there are more than ten people, break up the bigger group into smaller subgroups. Make sure the members are committed to participating each week, as this will help create stability and help you better prepare the structure of the meeting.

At the beginning of each week's study, start with the opening Getting Started question to introduce the topic you will be discussing. The members should answer briefly, as the goal is just for them to have an idea of the subject in their minds as you go over the lesson. This will allow the members to become engaged and ready to interact with the rest of the group.

After reviewing the lesson, try to initiate a free-flowing discussion. Invite group members to bring questions and insights they may have discovered to the next meeting, especially if they were unsure of the meaning of some parts of the lesson. Be prepared to discuss how biblical truth applies to the world we live in today.

WEEKLY PREPARATION

As the group leader, here are a few things that you can do to prepare for each meeting:

- *Be thoroughly familiar with the material in the lesson.* Make sure that you understand the content of each lesson so you know how to structure the group time and are prepared to lead the group discussion.

- *Decide, ahead of time, which questions you want to discuss.* Depending on how much time you have each week, you may not be able to reflect on every question. Select specific questions that you feel will evoke the best discussion.

- *Take prayer requests.* At the end of your discussion, take prayer requests from your group members and then pray for one another.

STRUCTURING THE DISCUSSION TIME

There are several ways to structure the duration of the study. You can choose to cover each lesson individually, for a total of twelve weeks of group meetings, or you can combine two lessons together per week, for a total of six weeks of group meetings. The following charts illustrate these options:

TWELVE-WEEK FORMAT

Week	Lessons Covered	Reading
1	Count It All Joy	James 1:1–8
2	Victorious in Trials	James 1:9–18
3	Doers of the Word	James 1:19–27
4	Dangerous Favoritism	James 2:1–7
5	A Faith with Integrity	James 2:8–17
6	Take Action!	James 2:18–26
7	Watch Your Words	James 3:1–12
8	Wisdom from Above	James 3:13–18
9	The Root of Conflicts	James 4:1–10
10	Planning Your Future	James 4:11–17
11	Justice and Endurance	James 5:1–11
12	Reasons to Pray	James 5:12–20

SIX-WEEK FORMAT

Week	Lessons Covered	Reading
1	Count It All Joy / Victorious in Trials	James 1:1–18
2	Doers of the Word / Dangerous Favoritism	James 1:19–2:7
3	A Faith with Integrity / Take Action!	James 2:8–26
4	Watch Your Words / Wisdom from Above	James 3:1–18
5	The Root of Conflicts / Planning Your Future	James 4:1–17
6	Justice and Endurance / Reasons to Pray	James 5:1–20

In regard to organizing your time when planning your group Bible study, the following two schedules, for sixty minutes and ninety minutes, can give you a structure for the lesson:

Section	60 Minutes	90 Minutes
Welcome: Members arrive and get settled	5 minutes	10 minutes
Getting Started Question: Prepares the group for interacting with one another	10 minutes	10 minutes
Message: Review the lesson	15 minutes	25 minutes
Discussion: Discuss questions in the lesson	25 minutes	35 minutes
Review and Prayer: Review the key points of the lesson and have a closing time of prayer	5 minutes	10 minutes

As the group leader, it is up to you to keep track of the time and keep things moving according to your schedule. If your group is having a good discussion, don't feel the need to stop and move on to the next question. Remember, the purpose is to pull together ideas and share unique insights on the lesson. Encourage everyone to participate, but don't be concerned if certain group members are more quiet. They may just be internally reflecting on the questions and need time to process their ideas before they can share them.

GROUP DYNAMICS

Leading a group study can be a rewarding experience for you and your group members—but that doesn't mean there won't be challenges. Certain members may feel uncomfortable discussing topics that they consider very personal and might be afraid of being called on. Some members might have disagreements on specific issues. To help prevent these scenarios, consider the following ground rules:

- If someone has a question that may seem off topic, suggest that it be discussed at another time, or ask the group if they are okay with addressing that topic.

- If someone asks a question you don't know the answer to, confess that you don't know and move on. If you feel comfortable, invite other group members to give their opinions or share their comments based on personal experience.
- If you feel like a couple of people are talking much more than others, direct questions to people who may not have shared yet. You could even ask the more dominating members to help draw out the quiet ones.
- When there is a disagreement, encourage the group members to process the matter in love. Invite members from opposing sides to evaluate their opinions and consider the ideas of the other members. Lead the group through Scripture that addresses the topic, and look for common ground.

When issues arise, encourage your group to think of Scripture: "Love one another" (John 13:34), "If it is possible, as much as it depends on you, live peaceably with all men" (Romans 12:18), and, "Be swift to hear, slow to speak, slow to wrath" (James 1:19).

ABOUT
Dr. David Jeremiah and Turning Point

Dr. David Jeremiah is the founder of Turning Point, a ministry committed to providing Christians with sound Bible teaching relevant to today's changing times through radio and television broadcasts, audio series, books, and live events. Dr. Jeremiah's teaching on topics such as family, prayer, worship, angels, and biblical prophecy forms the foundation of Turning Point.

David and his wife, Donna, reside in El Cajon, California, where he serves as the senior pastor of Shadow Mountain Community Church. David and Donna have four children and twelve grandchildren.

In 1982, Dr. Jeremiah brought the same solid teaching to San Diego television that he shares weekly with his congregation. Shortly thereafter, Turning Point expanded its ministry to radio. Dr. Jeremiah's inspiring messages can now be heard worldwide on radio, television, and the internet.

Because Dr. Jeremiah desires to know his listening audience, he travels nationwide holding ministry rallies and spiritual enrichment conferences that touch the hearts and lives of many people. According to Dr. Jeremiah, "At some point in time, everyone reaches a turning point; and for every person, that moment is unique, an experience to hold onto forever. There's so much changing in today's world that sometimes it's difficult to choose the right path. Turning Point offers people an understanding of God's Word and seeks to make a difference in their lives."

Dr. Jeremiah has authored numerous books, including *Escape the Coming Night* (Revelation), *The Handwriting on the Wall* (Daniel), *Overcoming Loneliness, What in the World Is Going On?, The Coming Economic Armageddon, I Never Thought I'd See the Day!, God Loves You: He Always Has—He Always Will, Agents of the Apocalypse, Agents of Babylon, Revealing the Mysteries of Heaven, People Are Asking . . . Is This the End?, A Life Beyond Amazing, Overcomer, The Book of Signs, Everything You Need,* and *Forward.*

New Bible Study Series from Dr. David Jeremiah

The Jeremiah Bible Study Series captures Dr. David Jeremiah's forty-plus years of commitment to teaching the whole Word of God. Each volume contains twelve lessons for individuals and groups to explore what the Bible says, what it meant to the people at the time it was written, and what it means to us today. Out of his lifelong ministry of *delivering the unchanging Word of God to an ever-changing world*, Dr. Jeremiah has written this Bible-strong study series focused not on causes, current events, or politics, but on the solid truth of Scripture.

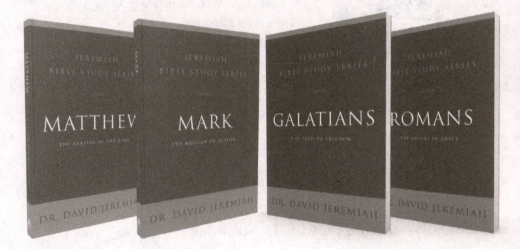

9780310091493	Matthew	9780310091554	John	9780310091646	1 Corinthians
9780310091516	Mark	9780310091608	Acts	9780310097488	2 Corinthians
9780310091530	Luke	9780310091622	Romans	9780310091660	Galatians

Available now at your favorite bookstore.
More volumes coming soon.

 THOMAS NELSON
Since 1798